HOW TO CUSTOMIZE
YOUR
HARLEY-DAVIDSON

Timothy Remus

Motorbooks International
Publishers & Wholesalers ®

First published in 1992 by Motorbooks International Publishers & Wholesalers, PO Box 2, 729 Prospect Avenue, Osceola, WI 54020 USA

Motorbooks International books are also available at discounts in bulk quantity for industrial or sales-promotional use. For details write to Special Sales Manager at the Publisher's address

Library of Congress Cataloging-in-Publication Data
Remus, Timothy.
   How to customize your Harley-Davidson / Timothy
     Remus.
         p.   cm.
   Includes bibliographical references and index.
   ISBN 0-87938-619-3
   1. Harley-Davidson motorcycle—Customizing. I.
     Title.
TL448.H3R46   1992
629.227′5—dc20   91-39509

On the front cover: *Form Vs. Function, the bike that is equally at home on the dragstrip and the street, as built by Donnie Smith for Willie Ditz. The cafe fairing is from Arlen Ness with the scallop paint job by Mallard Teal. The Evolution engine is truly a Big Twin at 93ci, built by Tator Gilmore and set in a stock Softail chassis.*

Printed and bound in the United States of America

Contents

Acknowledgments

I'm a strong believer in giving credit where credit is due. The acknowledgments are my way of saying thank you to people who helped with the book. So if this section is longer than most, it's because a number of people contributed to the researching and writing of this book.

First and foremost, I must thank Donnie Smith. It was in Donnie's shop that I photographed many a frame, engine and shock absorber. It was Donnie who answered about a million questions—and never called any of them dumb. And it was Donnie who looked at my early outline and proofread the final manuscript.

I also have to thank Peter Cottrell of D.S. Specialties for his good ideas, and Jim Ulasich of Eagle Engineering for his technical advice. Painter of note Mallard Teal shared his paint booth with me and answered almost as many questions as Donnie Smith. And Lenny Schwartz, also a painter, gave me the straight stuff on pinstriping.

Jon Kosmoski, one of the world's best-known painters and owner of House of Kolor, gave freely of his time and expertise. If everyone had as much enthusiasm for what they do as Jon has, the world would certainly be a better place.

I would be remiss if I forgot to thank Dan Stern at Custom Chrome, and Tom Motzko at Drag Specialties. It's all dollars and cents, I know, yet their enthusiasm for my project seemed to go beyond basic business.

Thanks, also, to Rick Ulrich at Crane Cams for help with the chapter on cam basics, and Pat Dunn from Performance Machine for sharing his expertise on brake systems.

For ideas for the book and ideas on the bikes I have to thank Arlen Ness. Arlen was always willing to take time to talk over the phone or sit over a cup of coffee in Sturgis.

Speaking of my friends among the local scooter-trash, Ron Banks and Jason Mitchell must be thanked for all their ideas and encouragement and for also proofreading the manuscript.

Thanks as well to Lee Chapin of Mikuni USA and Tom Butler of Custom Chrome for their assistance in the carburetor section.

My lovely and talented wife, Mary Lanz, must be thanked as well. For the last couple of weeks, all she's seen of me is the closed door to my office.

There's another group of people to thank whose names I have mostly forgotten. Men and women who work at companies like Crane and S&S and White Brothers and Sifton and Leineweber and a few others. It was encouraging to chat with these people; after talking with them it was obvious that they are working hard at building quality parts and taking good care of their customers.

Introduction

When Motorbooks asked me to write a Harley customizing book, I felt both flattered and frightened. Flattered at being asked, and frightened at the thought of what it would take to write a really good customizing manual for Harleys.

Writing a good book, first of all, would mean providing the reader with as much good technical information as possible. Second, that information would have to be presented in a style that could be understood and enjoyed by both first-time and experienced builders.

And that is exactly what I have tried to do: pack the book with as much quality information as possible. The information itself was obtained from the

Ron Banks wanted a low, lean, modern machine. Built entirely at home, this yellow FXR is based on a Harley frame, raked to about 37 degrees and completely molded. Ron achieved the low look and feel by cutting the front tubes two inches, installing shorter rear shocks and moving the upper shock mount forward. The Ness fenders and cafe-style fairing give the bike its modern appearance. Details include a chrome air cleaner and side covers, painted body color in the center, with the same graphics used throughout the bike.

5

best builders, painters and mechanics I could find. Professionals like Mallard Teal and Jim Ulasich and a dozen others who were open about sharing the things they have learned during a lifetime laboring at their craft.

Yet, even with a vast pool of quality information to present, other problems appeared. One is the matter of taste. People in different parts of the country have different ideas about how a Harley should look. For some, it's a Shovelhead in a hardtail frame and a long springer stretching way out front. Others want FXRs, low and sleek, painted in the latest neon colors.

In response to this dilemma I have tried to present a variety of suggestions for customizing, claiming that no one is better than another. And if there is a tilt, it's a tilt to the modern Harley—FXRs and Softails decorated in a modern style. Not because they are better, but because so much has already been written about the older styles. If the information in this book is going to be new, then it must be about new bikes and current trends.

Though some of the bikes and examples illustrated in this book are full-on radical bikes from professional builders like Donnie Smith, my intent is not to write a guide to building a show bike. It is to aid and inspire the home builder; the person who wants his or her Harley to look different—and

better—than it did stock. I hope to give some insight to anyone building what I call a Main Street Harley, a bike that relies on a mostly-stock frame, without many hand-fabricated parts. A bike built primarily by the owner, using mostly off-the-shelf parts.

Building an exceptional Harley requires a variety of skills, some good taste, a certain amount of cash and a good attitude. A proper attitude will carry the builder through the low points—all the way to the end of the project. But a book alone cannot instill those skills. A book cannot provide encouragement on that bad day when the whole project looks doomed.

There are, however, a few things a book *can* do. Skills are learned and earned—certainly a personal possession to take pride in. By providing technical information and how-to sections, I hope you will try to "do it yourself" and thereby learn that new skill. The pictures of finished bikes and bikes under construction are intended to provide lots of ideas, to inspire you to take on the challenge of building a better Harley, do it in good taste and avoid the normal first-time-builder blunders.

So, read and enjoy. But don't just leave it at that. Build that better bike, a motorcycle that is your very own.

Chapter 1

Planning Your Customizing

Customized Defined

Since the subject of this book is customizing motorcycles, it seems as if we should start with a definition of the word customized. *Webster's* defines customize as follows: " . . . to build, fit, or alter according to individual specifications." If I were to offer a definition, it might read something like this: The act of changing a thing (usually an automobile or motorcycle) for the purpose of enhanced visual appeal; after World War II, many young men customized their Fords and Mercurys.

A customized bike is one that somehow looks different from others of the same make and model. More than just different, most people set out to create a bike that looks better than those less desirable and more ordinary, stock motorcycles. So for us, the word customize will mean modifying a stock motorcycle to make that motorcycle look and run better than it did when stock.

Who Needs a Plan?

Customizing your Harley at first seems like a simple process of disassembly, purchasing of parts,

Bud reports that the fenders were the hardest part of the project. Built by Spin's Custom, the fiberglass fenders are shipped in raw form and take a lot of hand finishing. The massive Harley fork and multiple lights work well with the Indian fender. The Indian-head fender accessory is a very nice touch.

Built by Bud Beireis of Bud's Harley-Davidson, this Harley looks suspiciously like an old Indian. Bud chose the Indian look to achieve that one-of-a-kind look. The rigid frame is from Santee, the front fork from Harley-Davidson. Gas tanks are stock Harley units. Fenders and two-tone paint really make the Indian theme work. Details like the Indian logo on the tank and the Indian air cleaner reinforce the message.

Harley-Davidson Customizing 101

The history of customizing Harley-Davidsons probably started when one of the first young Harley-Davidson owners repainted his or her 1910 Harley V-twin. Americans love to tinker with their machines and no doubt there were modified and "improved" Harleys from the very beginning.

Yet, the beginning of customized motorcycles as discussed in this book really started in the 1960s with the birth of "choppers," or motorcycles stripped and chopped to the bare machine.

In the Beginning There Was the Chopper

The idea was simple: start with your basic Pan-head or Knucklehead, strip off the front fender, bob or trim the back fender and add a smaller gas tank. These were the days of *Easy Rider* when customizing had nothing to do with functionality or rideability. As time went on a certain style evolved, based on a rigid frame with a short springer fork, a Sportster gas tank and high bars or "ape hangers."

Once the chopper movement really caught on things moved rapidly and a variety of styles became popular. Springer forks were still considered the best, though some riders built their bikes with hydraulic forks. Whether hydraulic or springer, the forks got dramatically longer and the fork angle went from conservative to far-out.

Sportsters took on a life of their own, and in some parts of the country a Sportster was the *only* bike to ride. These Sportsters usually featured a raked frame, long springer or girder front end and struts instead of shock absorbers in the rear—rigidness has always been right up there next to godliness. Diamond-shaped gas tanks, known under a variety of names, appeared first on the West Coast and spread rapidly east.

Factory Customs

Willie G. Davidson was keenly aware of the action on Main Street, and in 1971 Harley-Davidson introduced the Super Glide. An astute move on the part of Harley-Davidson, the Super Glide carried the FL frame and an FX, or Sportster, fork. The first factory custom from Harley-Davidson, the Super Glide rapidly evolved to Low Rider, Fat Bob and Wide Glide.

We now had two kinds of customized bikes: those from the factory and those that were built by small shops and individuals. A lot of hybrid motorcycles were created and a customized bike could be anything from a radical chopper to a Low Rider with pearl paint. Riders went so far as to customize bikes of European or even *Oriental* descent (pure blasphemy). FLH Harleys were still stripped, but when they were reassembled the hydraulic fork was reinstalled, as were the factory fenders and gas tanks.

By the early 1980s, there was a serious change on the street. A quiet funeral service was held for choppers. It seemed that one day the streets were full of stretched, rigid frames and ape hanger handle bars, and the next day there were none. The stores that did such a great trade in long forks and tiny little peanut gas tanks shifted gears and began to sell more maintenance items. The bikes these shops maintained were often Super Glides, Low Riders and Wide Glides—the factory customs of the day.

Rebirth of the Customs

The rebirth of customized motorcycles started in the middle of the 1980s. About the same time Americans were rediscovering all their motorized toys; worries about finding enough gasoline seemed a thing of the past and modified cars as well as modified bikes came rolling out of America's garages.

Everyone seemed to get caught up in the action. The smell of high octane was in the air and everyone wanted a hit. Cars and motorcycles were great, especially if they were *American*. By this time, Harley-Davidson had cemented its reputation for quality; The Motor Company and its motorcycles were here to stay. People came to realize that these American motorcycles no longer dripped oil on the driveway and you didn't need to be a mechanic to ride a new Harley.

If the Low Rider or Wide Glide wasn't wild enough for you, well Harley had a new Softail model—a bike that combined the look of the old rigid-framed Harleys with the new Evolution engine, and many people bought a Harley for the first time. Others bought a Softail because it looked like the bike they used to have or the bike their Dad used to ride. Harley sales grew and the desire to customize these motorcycles grew as well. Everyone wanted a Harley, but everyone wanted theirs to look unique.

Traditionalists could have a Softail, modified to suit their tastes. More modern riders could buy an FXR and alter it with styling cues borrowed from Arlen Ness.

This new movement wasn't just choppers revisited; these new bikes differ in many ways from the earlier customized Harleys. The biggest difference is the emphasis on function first and form second. Yes, everyone wants a wild, customized Harley, but now they want that wild machine to work on a day-to-day basis.

A New Customizing Philosophy

Maybe it's because the riders are older; older men and women tend to make more realistic decisions. They understand the need for good brakes and good suspension. These riders want power, but they insist on good reliability too. A bike that requires lengthy maintenance sessions once a week has little appeal. Performance, in the larger sense of the word, has become a stated goal in most customizing projects.

Maybe the reason the new customized bikes work so much better than the old ones is because the bikes that the builders use as a starting point are so much better than the bikes we started on twenty years ago. All the bikes carry disc brakes, all have good suspension (on both ends), all have the new and much improved Evolution engine.

The future offers more of the same—bikes that look great and run just as well. Softails with rubber-mount frames, FXRs low and mean, both with a new repaint and reassembly. In fact, most people think the process is so simple that they just "do it." When someone suggests that they make out a detailed plan before picking up the wrenches or the parts catalog, they react with shock.

Planning the modifications may make it seem as if you're just "reading the directions," an unnecessary step that gets in the way of the real work—and fun—at hand, and stifles creativity. Yet, we have all seen too many bikes sporting lots of expensive chrome accessories and trick paint that are more eyesores than art forms—where mismatched parts get in the way of what might have been a good idea. Motorcycles that fail to ring the bell because there is no harmony in their design.

Everyone has their own word or phrase to describe a great bike. Some will call it bitchin', or cool. Other riders describe a great bike as having an attitude. One friend of mine simply calls it, "that

This mock-up, or drawing to scale, shows how a simple cardboard cutout was used by bike builder Donnie Smith to represent the tail section. Note that the small flip at the end was eliminated in the final design. A mock-up is both a means of evaluating the shape and (if the shape seems like a good idea) a representation of what the part will eventually look like. Many mock-ups go through a number of generations before the final shape is determined.

Arlen Ness advises builders to take time in mocking up a bike. In particular, Arlen likes to be sure the fender sits just right, with the radius of the fender running parallel to the radius of the wheel whenever possible. Pictured is one of Arlen's Tail Dragger fenders. The long tail on the fender helps to pull the whole bike closer to the ground, another of those visual tricks.

Eventually the mock-up is transferred to metal. In this case, the final shape of the metal is pretty close to the shape of the mock-up.

The finished, pro-street Harley. The go-fast look is provided by the aluminum wheels, the fat rear tire, the fairing and the air dam. As a final touch, the rear sheet metal was designed to resemble the bodies built around full-time drag race bikes.

look," assuming that you and I will understand what he means.

What it all boils down to is that a bike looks good when its parts and paint job work together to create their own beauty and style—whether simple and classy or moderately ornate.

Built by Don Hotop, this Sporty shows that Sportsters don't have to be short and squat. An extended frame and long, slim gas tank give it a nice slender profile. You can see the nicely polished cases and the ventilation slots in the sprocket cover. Built a few years ago, this bike goes to show that a good design has staying power and never really goes out of style.

Your success or failure in modifying your motorcycle depends on more than money or your skill as a mechanic. The success of your project depends on your ability to think things through. Your ability to design an attractive package on two wheels. One that looks good, that looks different from all the rest, and that is uniquely yours.

The easiest way to ensure your success is to think first and do later. Thoroughly planning the project ahead of time will help minimize the risk that your bike will be one of those eyesores, where all the money in the world won't make a sexy motorcycle.

Basically, a good plan will help you get the bike you want, without any surprises at the end; help ensure that the money you spend will be spent wisely and not wasted; and help you create a bike that is a "whole" design, with each part working along with the others in harmony.

This may be the most important part of the project. It is much easier to just start ordering parts. The temptation is to assume we know what we want to do and rush off to do it. Taking the time to work through a plan and follow it through is much harder, though ultimately much wiser in the end.

Making Out the Plan

Your plan for a new, customized Harley should reflect the kind of bike you really want. If you like to tour and can only afford one bike, then it has to be something that's comfortable on the highway. Riders who prefer short hops and cruising on main street will want a different kind of bike. For them, comfort can take a back seat to style. Be honest with yourself—what kind of riding do you do, and how will the new bike be used?

Built in the Arlen Ness shop, this Softail gets maximum effect from well-chosen accessories, plenty of chrome and some very nice paint. The frame has been molded and painted. The chrome fender rails mount the Streamliner rear fender. Polished rotors, spoked wheels and polished lower fork legs round out the details.

The ultimate use for the bike, as well as your budget, will help decide what type of engine modifications to plan as well. Touring riders will favor mild modifications in order to keep the engines as dependable as possible. Riders who prefer to barhop may insist on serious horsepower—dependability be damned!

Putting together a plan for your new bike might start with a worksheet stating what features the basic bike has and exactly what modifications you plan to make. Once you list each change, you can write in cost and time estimates for each modification. If you work at your job twelve hours a day, six days a week there won't be time to construct a really wild bike unless you farm out most of the work. If the amount of income you can dedicate to the new bike project is minimal, it would be a waste of time to plan a killer bike with an expensive motor and hand-formed panels.

Whether or not you plan to remove the engine will have a major impact on your project. If you intend to build a mild bike without frame modifications, the engine can be left in the frame. The downside to leaving the engine in the frame is that you cannot paint the frame. Since most frames are black, not painting the frame means you have to choose a paint scheme that will work with a black frame.

During the planning stage you should start a file called "Bikes I like." Look through all your old scooter-trash magazines and pick out the bikes that really catch your eye. Next, collect all the bike

Mike Addiss assembled his Panhead using a timeless theme. The Tombstone taillight, simple seat with pillion pad, shotgun pipes and bright flames make it look like an old Harley should. The missing carburetor is on the other side, bolted to a belt-driven blower.

The centerpiece of Bob Walters' FXR, the gas tank has seen extensive handwork. The subtle arch that runs along the bottom of the tank adds to the design of the whole bike. There is also a small (and hard to see) "dashboard" molded into the top of the tank. Because the gas tank is such a relatively large part of a motorcycle, its size and shape have a major impact on the overall design.

At first, this Bob Walters-built Harley seems like a nice, clean FXR. The fenders are from Arlen Ness, as is the cafe-style fairing. A closer look reveals the little things that were done to make this bike stand out. Things like a sidedraft Dell'Orto carburetor, outstanding paint job, great graphics and a very special tank.

The success of the Fat Boy has spawned a new generation of custom, ultra Fat Boys. This example, from Arlen Ness, features his Tail Dragger fenders, chrome swing arm and chrome rear fender rail. Who says cafe fairings only belong on FXRs and Ninjas? This Fat Boy also features forward controls and dual exhaust.

photos that you have taken at shows, Sturgis or Daytona and pick out the best ones. Then spread them out on a table or across the floor. Separate the photos into Best, OK and Not-so-great categories.

Now take the Best-bikes pile and pick out the ones that fit your type of riding. If some of the OK bikes are missing just a few details compared to the Best category, think about what the missing details are. If the bikes were yours, what would you change that would qualify them for the Best category?

This detail monster is the brain child of Donnie Smith. It would be hard to put this unusual-looking bike into any one category. The look is long, accentuated by the radical fork angle. This bike seemed to be the "people's favorite" in Sturgis, South Dakota.

The custom bike world has changed considerably in the last ten years. This nicely built and detailed Sportster (with a big twin transmission) features the mandatory long springer fork and minimal front brake. Today's bikes tend to be more functional than those of years past. Current builders stress the importance of dual disc brakes, quality suspension on both ends and less radical frame geometry.

Patty's Sportster is a good example of the "do it with paint and a few well-chosen accessories" concept. The bike features two-tone paint with graphics across the tank, small fairing and simple seat. The chrome fender rail and shotgun pipes add a little extra sparkle.

Lenny Schwartz stripped his 1968 Sportster to the frame and rebuilt it for the 1990s. He took four inches of stretch out of the frame and then began reassembling his "new" Sportster. The rebuild included using an Arlen Ness fairing, modern graphics and a Streamliner rear fender. Retained are a few vestiges of the bike's earlier life, like the spun-aluminum oil tank and longer-than-stock frame.

As you spend time analyzing the different features and designs of various bikes, you will become a better critic and come to see which bike designs work for you. At the same time, you will be able to decide more specifically what style and function you want, and why.

Sketching Out the Bike

The exact way in which you put together the plan for your new bike will depend on your background and skill. Noted customizer Arlen Ness doesn't like to sketch out a bike beforehand. He explains: "I just kind of put the bike together in my head; of course, I've been doing it for a lot of years. The bikes almost always come out the way I thought they would.

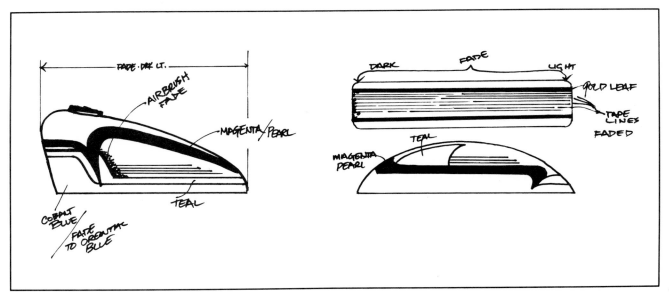

Some plans are more elaborate than others. This detailed sketch was done by Lenny Schwartz of Krazy Kolors in St. Paul, Minnesota, for the paint and graphics on his

Sportster. Your sketch doesn't have to be this nice; the idea is to come up with a good, solid concept of what the bike will look like when it's finished.

13

Sometimes the bike is better than I thought it would be, but I really never get one that's a big disappointment."

Unless your design skills are on a par with Arlen's, a more thoughtful planning process is probably called for. If you have any drawing skills, take pencil to paper and make a sketch of what the new bike will look like. If that seems too tough, do a tracing from a current photo of the bike, and then sketch in your changes. Even if your sketches don't look like something Picasso would have created, the process will help you to visualize what the finished bike should look like.

A copy machine and a set of colored pencils or markers can be a great aid at this point. Just run off a picture of the bike on the copy machine (enlarge it as much as possible) and then use the copies as a starting point for your design work. Cut and paste to your heart's content. Want more rake? Just cut off the fork and wheel and then paste them back on at any angle you like. With a scissors, a razor knife and some Elmer's glue, you can create any profile you want. Make it lower, longer, shorter or fatter. Once you have a profile, or basic shape, it's time to think about color.

Before talking about color, though, there are a few basic facts to get out of the way. A lot of riders

This slick, very 1990s kind of custom is the brain child of Peter Cottrell of DS Specialties in Minneapolis, Minnesota. Based on an old Shovelhead, there's little of the original bike left. The Shovel became an Evo when an Evolution top end was used on the Shovelhead flywheels and cases. The rest of the bits and pieces come from a variety of unusual sources. The wheels are from Performance Machine, plated for extra sparkle, the fenders were hand built, the tanks are special items from Arlen Ness, the exhaust is from Jardine. The bright green neon paint was applied by Jon Kosmoski, owner of House of Kolor in Minneapolis, Minnesota.

Racing forward into the past—two interpretations of the chopper theme. The Knucklehead in the background is closer to reality then; the Panhead in the foreground is closer to reality now. Note the molded-in lights, and the air scoop from an old AA-Fueler. Flames seem to work in any time period.

Some designs are more radical than others.

paint their bikes black. Black is fine, but it's also boring and makes your ride look like every other bike parked at the curb. Bike builder Donnie Smith tells the story of planning a new bike for a friend of his: "We had it all figured out, a wild Shovelhead with a chrome fork, lots of anodizing and engraving, a really nice bike. Finally, I asked him what color he had chosen for the new bike. When he said black, I said I didn't even want to build the bike."

Watch the people walking down the street at Sturgis, Daytona or the local ABATE chapter picnic. The bike that gets a second or third look, the one that draws a crowd, is the bike with a great paint job, one that helps the bike make a statement. So, if you don't like attention, if you don't want any magazine reporters to take a picture of your bike and if you don't want to attract members of the opposite sex, then paint that sucker black like the inside of a cow.

This is where the colored pencils come in handy. Experiment with different colored pencils (but throw the black one away). Paint that bike pink, green, yellow or some combination. Make several copies of your bike sketch and paint each one a different color. Which one looks best? Which color seems best suited to your design?

You won't be able to get the exact color you want with pencils or markers, so once you have the selection narrowed down, talk to a professional painter or paint supplier. Examine color charts, and ask for help if you can't decide which tone to choose. If you intend to have the bike pinstriped by a professional, talk to the pinstriper now. A good striper knows a lot about colors and color combinations.

Once you have decided on the basic form of the bike and you know what color or colors it's going to

Built by Al Reichenbach, this custom scooter shows a number of unique features: a black paint job that works better than most due to the engraving and detail work, a blower mounted on the right side, flattened tanks, and flat-black exhaust.

be, it's time to think about the details and accessories—if you haven't already. Ideas abound in the latest catalogs from Custom Chrome, Drag Specialties and Arlen Ness. Page through for ideas, making a list of all the goodies you want and their prices. Make sure the goodies you choose complement each other and fit in with the theme for the

The same, only different. Two FXRs, both modern, both yellow, yet very different. In the foreground, Gene's bike features a monochromatic paint job with limited chrome. Note the unique way the gas tank meets the frame. In the background, Ron Banks' bike uses more chrome and mounts the tank in the conventional fashion.

If you think all FXR customs look alike, check out this example built by Cory Ness. The long and low look is exaggerated by stretching the frame and adding to the fork angle. The paint, shades of blue against a black background, works in harmony with the wheels. The overall look is very clean, fast and uncluttered.

A nearly stock Softail—before. This bike has been lowered and the rear fender has been extended slightly to exaggerate the lowered look. The pipes are stock. This is just a real clean Fat Boy.

bike. A high-tech FXR, for instance, will need different accessories than a nostalgia-style Softail. Try not to mix chrome parts with the new billet look. Stay with your theme.

The Worksheet

As the design and style of the bike starts to take form, think seriously about how much it will cost and how long it will take to build. Be honest in assessing your own skills and deciding how much

A not-so-stock Softail—after. In reality, this bike has changed very little. The front fender has been extended slightly like the rear and painted white. The tank has been scalloped in white over the factory black with "shadows" done in a third color. Tom Radd, owner and builder of this Softail, builds street rods for a living. In fact, street rodders have an abundance of good ideas that might be used on custom Harleys.

Clippings from old magazines, along with your favorite snapshots can be combined into a collection of your favorite bikes. By spending some time looking over the photos you can better identify the designs and features you like. A few brainstorming sessions like this will make it easier to do a good job of planning that new Harley-Davidson.

work will have to be farmed out to painters, fabricators and mechanics. If this is your first Harley and your mechanical aptitude ranks rather low, don't assume that you can rebuild the motor at home—without any help and without any tools.

Following are three examples of worksheets you might create for your own project. They represent three ways of building a custom motorcycle, from mild to wild. The bike is assumed to be a late-model FXR in basically good mechanical condition. By expanding on the worksheets, actual costs can be determined—depending on how much of the work the owner plans to do at home.

Stage 1

The Stage 1 bike is basically stock, easy for anyone to build. All parts are readily available. The

Not just your wish books, catalogs like these can help in planning the new bike. They'll give you an idea of what is available and what it will cost.

A fresh approach to an old FX Shovelhead—by Donnie Smith. Note the molded-in fender rails, license plate bracket and taillight. The Shovel's small front fender, dual disc brakes, Ness fairing and bobbed rear fender all work together to make the bike appear fresh and fast. The frame is stock Harley-Davidson with a little extra rake. Cast, spoked wheels painted body color add a nice touch.

only part of the project that the builder might farm out is the paint work.

Component	Modification
Frame	Stock, no paint
Shocks and fork	Stock
Brakes	Stock
Engine	Stock, add S&S or Screamin' Eagle air cleaner assembly
Exhaust system	Basically stock, drill out baffles in factory pipes

One of Donnie Smith's personal rides, this FXR has been lowered at the front and rear by cutting the tubes and installing shorter shocks. The frame is molded and raked; the front forks feature polished lower legs and dual disk brakes. The paint is red with gold scrollwork on the fairing, tank and side covers. From this angle the extra rake combined with the fairing makes the bike look as though it's stretched out and ready to go.

Accessories	Arlen Ness side covers; chrome one-piece license plate mount; chrome cookie for rear belt sprocket
Paint work	Single-color paint job with pinstriping and accents

With the Stage 1 bike, the owner first must determine whether to farm it out to a professional painter or do the work himself or herself. If the

This very clean 1984 FL is another of Bud Beireis' motorcycles. He left it mostly stock, lowering the bike slightly and sending it to Kevin Winters for a blue and white paint job. The dual discs were added with the help of a 1988 fork.

Another Donnie Smith-built FXR. This one is more like a Stage 1 bike than a Stage 3. The bike has been lowered, but the frame remains stock. Fenders and gas tank are also stock. Major changes include the Ness fairing and side covers, and the red paint job with subtle graphics.

17

Simple, basic and black. This recent Arlen Ness bike features his five-speed, rubber mount frame, dual-rail

swing arm and Performance Machine brakes. Paint is black on black with just a few chrome accessories.

A very successful Stage 1 bike. Steve Lautug wanted a thoroughly modern Softail—one he could ride while he built the other, more radical ride. The sheet metal is stock; the biggest difference is the paint job, done in peach with yellow inserts and trim. The look is 1950s, complete with fishtail pipes and whitewall tires. Just like the lead sleds of 1953, this Softail has been lowered— almost two inches on either end—with White Brothers kits. A lot was achieved here without a complete disassembly of the bike.

painting will be done at home, then the cost of the paint and materials, along with the cost of the accessories, will give an accurate cost figure for the job. Be realistic when figuring the time needed to do the work. A good formula might be: estimated time to do the work multiplied by two to equal actual time needed.

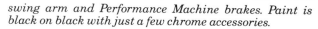

Some things never change. A. D. Meyer's Panhead looks just as good today as it did thirty years ago. Mike Urseth

Stage 2

The Stage 2 bike will take more time and money to complete. It is what you might call a serious street motorcycle. While the Stage 1 bike required only that you disassemble it far enough to do the paint job, the Stage 2 bike will require a complete disassembly in order to paint the frame.

Component	Modification
Frame	New paint, no molding
Shocks and fork	New, 11in chrome gas shocks; fork lowered with White Brothers kit
Brakes	Create dual discs with addition of new lower fork leg, second caliper (with caliper mounting boss) and disc
Engine	Mild hop-up: Stock carburetor, domed air cleaner (matches derby cover), mild cam with new rollers for lifters and new adjustable pushrods, shaved heads for more compression
Exhaust system	SuperTrapp two-into-one system
Accessories	Arlen Ness side covers; chrome cookie for rear belt sprocket; new domed derby cover with Allen screws; new taillight assembly; stealth mirrors and levers
Paint work	Two-tone paint job with scallops across the small fairing and the tank, scallops will be pinstriped

The Stage 2 bike is a serious project, if for no other reason than because it requires complete disassembly of the motorcycle so the frame can be painted. If the paint work is farmed out, the cost becomes considerable.

Coordination becomes important, too, so the work done by outside shops is finished at about the same time. When figuring the time required to have someone else do the paint or engine work, beware of those times of the year (like pre-Daytona or pre-Sturgis) when all the shops are very busy.

Stage 3

The Stage 3 bike is a truly customized motorcycle requiring complete disassembly and a major investment of time and money by the owner. The Stage 3 bike is not your garden-variety custom motorcycle. It is the product of an experienced builder of Harley-Davidsons, or someone with the budget to hire high-buck labor.

Component	Modification
Frame	Molded, raked an additional 4 degrees and painted
Shocks and fork	New, Magnumatic gas shocks;

The Fat Boy Softails have spawned a whole series of ultra Fat Boys. This Donnie Smith rendition carries Arlen's widest Tail Dragger fenders, five-gallon Fat Bob tanks from Harley-Davidson and a great scallop paint job in pink and blue by professional bike painter Mallard Teal of St. Paul, Minnesota. The success of this bike lies in the clever use of off-the-shelf parts, good attention to detail and a wonderful paint job. Look for more of these big, comfortable, colorful Harleys in the future.

Component	Modification
	front fork lowered with White Brothers kit; polished lower legs
Swing arm	New, adjustable chrome swing arm
Brakes	Polished Performance Machine calipers (dual discs in front),

Anyone who says black bikes are boring (like me, for example) must make an exception for a bike like Al Reichenbach's FXR. The black contrasts nicely with the gold—yes, gold—trim used throughout the bike, including the barrels, and the engraving and scrollwork on the tank and fenders.

Can a motorcycle be elegant? This FXR is nicely balanced and exhibits a lot of class. The spoked wheels, polished engine and wonderful paint job by Horst add up to a stunning package.

Component	Modification
	large-diameter floating rotors, polished front master cylinder
Wheels	Mitchell spun-aluminum wheels, new tires
Engine	Stock displacement, S&S carb and air cleaner, strong street camshaft with adjustable pushrods and new lifters, shaved heads with mild porting, single-fire ignition
Exhaust system	Drag pipes or staggered duals with antireversion cones
Accessories	Chrome side covers; aftermarket front and rear fenders and taillight assembly; cafe fairing; air dam; chrome cookie for rear sprocket; aftermarket chrome belt guard; customized gas tank with

Another approach to the performance look. This Sportster rides on a very long, hardtail chassis with custom gas tank, ultra-fat rear rubber and large air dam.

Component	Modification
	Ninja-style gas cap; aftermarket seat
Paint work	Single-color paint job for frame and body panels, multicolor flames on gas tank

A complete worksheet for the Stage 3 bike will probably be two or three pages long. Expenses will include the cost of frame work and the cost of at least the flamed part of the paint job. You will want to be careful about who does your engine work and porting. Be sure to allow enough time to have all these outside services performed.

If this is to be your first customized Harley, you might not have a good idea what it would cost to build the new bike. Many riders start off with a wish list—their own version of the Stage 3 bike. Then after checking into and adding up the cost of each modification or accessory, they opt for something closer to the Stage 1 or 2 customizing, something closer to real life. The point is, you won't know what it's going to cost until you itemize each part of the project and tally it up.

Designing Your Design

As you consider the type of bike you're going to build and the kind of accessories it will carry, there are a few more things to think about. First, remember that sometimes less is more. A good design doesn't need a blinding light to attract attention—it might only need subtle accents or highlights.

Second, keep in mind that what's really hot today may be old and cold by tomorrow. Neon paint and pink graphics might be fine today, but two years from now the look might be so dated that you'll need to repaint the bike.

Third, you don't have to do the same thing as everyone else. Consider your plans carefully, and spend a little time with pencil and paper to make sure the new bike is going to look great—and then go for it!

Fourth, once you have a plan, avoid any tendencies to change it. When you get to the point where you are nearly finished with your project, you might be tempted to substitute a part that is easier to install or cheaper than what was on your original list of accessories. The primary idea in making the plan was to ensure that all the parts would work together—don't sacrifice a good design just to save ten bucks or because there's a new fad in town.

Before finishing the planning part of the project, you should consider the difference between reality and illusion in the design of a vehicle. Much of what you see in a modified bike or car isn't real. That is, good designers use paint, chrome and highlights to trick the viewer's brain into thinking that a bike or car is longer, lower or wider than it really is. The living room of your house will probably appear bigger in white than it would in blue. The room is obvi-

Arlen Ness
The Master Customizer

Among all the Harley builders there is one man who is better known than any other. One name that is recognized the world over as the best known of all the bike builders. That man, that name, is Arlen Ness. After almost thirty years of building custom motorcycles, Arlen Ness has reached the very top.

Getting to the top isn't easy, especially if you have to climb there the old-fashioned way—with lots of sweat and hard work. Yet, Arlen climbed the stairs one custom Harley at a time. Each one different from the one before, most of them winners, all of them created in the mind of a very talented designer.

Arlen is a man with a variety of talents and abilities. Yet when you look over all the great motorcycles Arlen has built, there is one ability that stands out, one thing that makes all those bikes great. That one special ability is Arlen's talent for design.

Arlen's bikes always "flow." The bike, its handlebars, gas tank, wheels and fenders all somehow work together. There never seems to be a part that doesn't fit with the other parts or with the design and theme for the bike.

Arlen is also a man willing to take a risk. Willing and very able to break the mold. The result is a string of great two-wheeled designs. Each one different from those that went before, yet each one a winner, shaped by Arlen's keen sense of style and proportion.

Even a man with a special talent needs to go to school. For Arlen it was the school of hard knocks. His first experimenting was done on cars. His cars and his friends' cars were painted and changed and customized. Finally, the allure of two wheels was too much and Arlen brought home a used Knucklehead.

The first thing Arlen had to learn was how to ride a motorcycle. It wasn't much later that Arlen painted his first motorcycle, a certain Harley-Davidson Knucklehead. When Arlen parked the new paint job on Oakland's East Fourteenth Street, there were nods of approval among the onlookers. Soon people were asking if Arlen could do a "nice paint job like that for my bike."

Arlen quickly graduated from simple paint jobs to elaborate paint work combined with long, stretched tanks, custom fenders and handle bars of his own design. In fact, Arlen's Ramhorn handlebars were his first big commercial success.

Arlen remembers twenty years ago, about the time he opened his first small store. It was only open in the evenings, because Arlen still had his day job to hold down. What Arlen remembers best is coming down to open the store in the evening and finding people waiting outside, waiting to buy a pair of those new handlebars.

The Ramhorn bars were only the first in a long string of great Arlen Ness designs. Inspired by the drag racers, Arlen started building bikes with long, angular tanks. Arlen, and the other aftermarket companies, sold a lot of those tanks.

There have been phases in the bike building, supercharger phases followed by a turbocharger period followed by more blowers. Arlen has a knack for taking a big piece like a blower—one with a lot of visual appeal—and integrating it into the total design for the bike. The result is a machine almost larger than life.

Trying to pick out the best from among Arlen's many bikes is a tough call. Where do you start? With the early Knucklehead that sits now in the Oakland Museum? The bike has a 100ci engine force fed by a Magnuson blower mated to a Sportster transmission. Or maybe we should consider *Two Bad*, the twin-engine bike with torsion bar front suspension, the engines used as a stressed member, and oil and gas tanks integrated into the custom body work.

Arlen's most recent wild-ride, the very red Ferrari bike, features a John Harmon V-Twin with two blowers, two nitrous-oxide bottles and four sidedraft carburetors—all enclosed by full body work hammered out by Craig Naff at Boyd Coddington's shop. The special red paint was mixed up specially by Jon Kosmoski at House of Kolor as a favor to Arlen.

Bolting enormous blowers and nitrous bottles on a Harley-Davidson is one thing. Assembling a wild bike that has great lines and enormous visual impact is something else entirely. The secret to Arlen's success isn't a secret—it's a talent for design, nurtured over the years, combined with a lot of hard work.

Arlen Ness, the best known of the professional Harley builders, has been building bikes for more than twenty years. During that time Arlen has earned a reputation for good design and for consistently introducing new ideas to the motorcycle market.

Main street, Sturgis, South Dakota, early 1980s. Times have changed. There are more Harleys now than ever, and they get nicer every year.

ously the same size, the difference is in your head. In the same way, a bike will look longer and lower if there are some horizontal stripes or graphics running through the paint from one end to the other.

Strong vertical members—a large sissy bar is an extreme example—make a bike look short and stocky. Unbroken lines running from front to back make bikes look longer than they really are. Learning how to use all these design cues takes years. The key for new builders is to at least understand that these styling concepts exist, and to begin thinking about them. Choosing paint and pinstriping is more than just a matter of picking colors that you like. It's a matter of choosing colors

and combinations that make the bike look good—colors and combinations that enhance your total design.

Planning for Quality

There is one more thing to plan for: quality. One of the differences between a bike that's great and one that's just OK, is the detail. Anyone can bang together a bike or hang some chrome goodies on a new scooter. It takes attention to detail to create a *special* bike. A bike that looks as good at three feet away as it does at ten feet. When people move in close to have a better look at your bike, you don't want to start apologizing because the bolts are rusty or because that small bracket you welded to the chain guard never got painted.

Great machines don't just happen. They are built by individuals who take enormous pride in what they do. Mechanical skills are learned, attention to detail is an attitude. This may be your first bike project, but that doesn't mean you can't do neat work and develop good attention to detail. Even though you might be on a tight budget (aren't we all?), that shouldn't affect the quality of the work you do. When you plan the project, plan to hold yourself to a very high standard—to do the very best work you know how.

Though sanding, painting and assembling might seem the toughest part of building a bike, the planning step is probably the most difficult. Building a real killer bike requires that you truly know what you want, and understand how to get it. A good plan doesn't require an outlay of cash, it only requires your thought and your time—time that is very well spent.

At one time or another, nearly everything imaginable has been tried.

22

Chapter 2

Disassembly

Disassembling a motorcycle may seem like the simplest thing in the world. After all, who needs help tearing something apart? In just one Saturday afternoon, you and a friend can have that bike completely ripped apart. Seven or eight hours later you can look with satisfaction at the bare frame, the engine in one corner, a pile of fenders and wheels in another. The trouble comes two or six months later when you start to reassemble the bike. Suddenly, you have no idea which bolts from among the many you removed hold on the front calipers. Worse, you may spend all your time looking for the brake hoses or the small crush washers that seal the hose to the caliper—instead of spending your time building the motorcycle.

Disassembly may *seem* the easiest part of the task. Builders should remember, however, that *how* the bike is disassembled will determine how easy it is to reassemble. By being neat and thinking ahead, you can make the reassembly a pleasant task rather than an enormous headache.

The idea is to stash the parts so you can find and identify them later. Some old cardboard boxes work well for the larger parts, and plastic Ziploc bags work great for smaller assortments of bolts and nuts.

Neatness Counts

When you tear apart that Harley in the garage, take a minute first to find some boxes and a felt-tip marker. As the fenders and large chunks come off the bike, put them in boxes and label each box. Organize the boxes in logical sequence. One might be labeled Front Fork, while another would be marked Rear Suspension. Small parts, nuts and bolts, washers and screws should go in Ziploc bags and then be placed in the correct box with the rest of the fenders or fork parts or whatever. When the disassembly is finished, put the boxes on the shelf so they don't get lost or kicked across the garage floor.

This way, there is no question as to which bolts were used for the calipers. And this way, you spend your time putting your new bike together, not looking for misplaced parts or wondering which bolt fits which hole.

How Far Is Too Far?

The time has come to take the bike apart. You've waited all summer for this. Finally, one Saturday morning when it's too cool to ride, you and a buddy

Cleanliness may not be next to godliness, but it does help the work flow smoothly—and neatly.

Donnie Smith
Background in Drag Racing

Donnie Smith is a man with many skills. Chief among those skills is his knack for building great custom Harleys. On Donnie's bikes, everything fits in both a mechanical and an aesthetic sense. Formerly part owner of the Smith Brothers and Fetrow shop in Minneapolis, Donnie Smith is currently a man doing just what he likes—building Harleys for special customers in his small shop.

Like Arlen Ness, Donnie is another man who started out with cars. As a young man he left the family farm in western Minnesota and came to "the cities" of Minneapolis and St. Paul. Four years after arriving Donnie was campaigning a Willys Gasser on the drag strip and fabricating parts for the other racers. In about 1971, he and his partners made a real business out of their racing and fabrication by opening Smith Brothers and Fetrow.

The shop was designed primarily to build race cars —and help the three partners pay for their own drag racing habit. Somehow they started doing a little motorcycle fabrication along with the car work. In a few years motorcycles and motorcycle projects occupied all the space in the shop. Eventually the race car was sold and the shop became a very successful fabrication and manufacturing facility. Almost fifteen years later, when the chopper and modified motorcy-

Donnie Smith, formerly part owner of the Smith and Fetrow shop in Minneapolis, Minnesota, is currently building bikes in his small shop. His recent projects include a Pro-Street bike, an ultra Fat Boy and the radical ride he built for himself.

cle market got soft, Donnie and his partners closed the store and moved on to other projects.

He credits his rural farm background as the place where he learned his basic mechanical skills. The ability to fix a broken combine or John Deere tractor was enhanced when Dad sent him to a special high school with a wide range of shop classes. Donnie was able to take the standard shop classes like engine overhaul and also some classes that would lay the foundation for later fabrication work. Sheet metal working and welding were certainly two classes that would prove useful to Donnie all through his life.

Donnie has a variety of good mechanical skills, although after watching him you begin to realize that he has an additional ability. When the discussion turns to how a certain piece should be built or fabricated, it becomes obvious that Donnie has a deep understanding of engineering. Not the numbers and the logarithms but an almost innate understanding of how stresses and loads are carried and distributed through a frame or a bracket. When Donnie holds a bracket or a mount in his hands it seems as though he can "feel" what the bracket will experience when placed under a load.

Years of building race cars where the weight must be low and the strength high, provided the experiences Donnie needed to hone his understanding of engineering. Later, as part owner of Smith Brothers and Fetrow, Donnie often designed the parts that were manufactured and sold under their name—not just brackets and accessories, but Donnie also designed girder front forks and complete frames.

Donnie's early bikes exhibit a certain flair. *Pandemonium*, built in 1978, was a full-on custom constructed almost entirely by hand. A wild Shovelhead with a Magnuson blower, it was the engineering and design details that made it an exciting bike. By making the engine a stressed member of the chassis, Donnie was able to eliminate the upper frame tube. The gas tank was located under the seat and the oil tank was incorporated into the rear fender.

Unveiled some thirteen years later, Donnie's most recent bike exhibits the same kind of clever engineering in a more sophisticated package. The new bike relies on a hand-built frame and swing arm and mostly hand-built sheet metal as well. The really innovative features start at the rear fender, wide enough to house the license plate within the fender. On the left side the fender flares out to cover the chain. The open primary reveals polished pulleys while everything else is painted to match the rest of the bike. The long, stretched gas tank matches the profile of the rest of the bike and carries a small hand built console with the mystery opening for the gas cap. The list of features goes on and on.

Donnie Smith has built another killer bike. Everything works, everything fits in both a mechanical and visual sense. Those classes in high school, the work building race cars and later motorcycles, have all paid off. The winners here are you and I, the riders who get to appreciate and learn from another man's skills.

start in with enthusiasm. When the question arises of how far you are going to take the bike apart, you decide to take it all the way down to the frame. That way, you figure you can get everything done right. You can paint the frame, you can rewire the bike, you can smooth out some of those ugly welds. There seem to be so many good reasons for taking the disassembly process all the way, you figure, why not?

This is one of those situations where common logic is flawed. Taking the bike all the way down to the frame may be a good idea if you are sure you're going to mold or paint the frame, you want to modify the frame or the bike has a lot of miles on it and truly needs a complete going over.

Too many people rip the bike apart without having a good idea of what they're doing or what their final goals are for the project. Many of the basket cases advertised for sale in the Sunday paper are the result of such misguided projects—projects that were easier to rip apart than they were to correctly reassemble. Remember, taking it apart is always easier than putting it back together.

So stick with your plan. If you are building a mild custom based on a late-model FXR, there's no need to rip everything apart. If your plan includes repainting the fenders, tank and side covers, take those off but leave the rest of the bike intact. If you intend to leave the frame black, settle for a good cleaning and a little touchup where the paint is chipped.

Pulling out that big factory wiring harness in favor of a "simpler" one built at home may not be such a good idea, either. If the harness has rubbed through in a couple of places, just repair the areas with bad insulation. Be sure to solder and carefully tape any repairs you make. Although a lot of those wires seem unnecessary, the Harley engineers just may know more about wiring and electrical systems than you do. Making Mickey Mouse repairs to an otherwise good wiring harness is a sure way to screw up the reliability of your motorcycle.

Initial Cleaning

There is one job that should be done just after disassembly and that is giving all parts a good cleaning. There's never going to be a better time to clean that frame or those engine cases or the hidden part of the swing arm. So buy a can of Gunk or a similar type of engine degreaser and start scrubbing. Spray on the Gunk and allow it to soak in for three to four minutes. A small wire brush or an old toothbrush will help loosen stubborn caked-on grease in corners and around bolts. Once you've got the big chunks off, use some strong soap and water to finish the job. Don't use gasoline or a flammable solvent for cleaning, no matter how convenient it seems at the time.

Parts Inventory

This is a good time to take an inventory of any worn-out parts that were discovered during the disassembly. Things like worn brake pads (if you're going to keep the factory brakes), cracked brackets and stripped and missing nuts. Make a list of the items you need and add it to the list of goodies you intend to buy for that new motorcycle.

Once the disassembly and cleaning are finished, it's a good time to take a long look at the total project. The list of parts to be ordered should be double-checked. Parts that will be sent out to the frame or chrome shop can be set aside, ready to drop off or ship out.

Be sure to allow enough time for the bottlenecks that occur in most projects. Painters and chrome shops don't always work as quickly as you'd like, so be sure to get a time estimate and then get your parts over to them as early as possible. Don't make the mistake of letting the swing arm you need chrome plated sit in your garage for two months, then rush it to the chrome shop pleading for a one-week turnaround.

And try to avoid the pre-Daytona or pre-Sturgis death march. Remember that most of the other men and women in town want their new bike completed at the same time you do. Try to schedule around the painter's busiest season so you're not in competition with ten other people to get your parts painted by mid-July. Remember, too, that your earlier resolve to do high-quality work may go completely to hell when you have to stay up all night three nights in a row just to get the bike done on time.

With the bike disassembled and cleaned, the project has taken one giant step forward. After a short break to check on the master plan, you can actually begin the best part of the whole project—bolting the new bike together.

Shelves, shelves and more shelves. You can't have too many in your shop. They make it possible to store the various parts in separate cubbyholes. They also make it possible to have two projects going at one time in the same garage without all the parts ending up in one big heap.

25

Chapter 3

Paint Preparation and Custom Painting

At the heart of every nice custom Harley is an exceptional paint job. While many bike builders send fenders and tanks out to be painted by professionals, there is no reason you can't paint your own bike. Especially if you are an individual long on time and short on money, or simply the kind of person who would rather do it yourself. Painting is a skill like any other. It requires attention to detail, good materials and good tools.

Though a multicolored, Candy flame job might not be a realistic goal for a first-time painter, a nice clean one-color, or even a base coat-Candy coat paint job can be done by the novice painter.

So, the purpose of this chapter is to encourage anyone with the inclination that you *can* do a good paint job at home. For those riders who would rather send their gas tanks and fenders out for painting, this chapter should help you to communicate better with their professional painter, and in making intelligent decisions regarding the choice of materials.

Unless you use an HVLP gun with its own turbine, you will be relying on your air compressor as the heart of your painting system. Though this 5hp commercial compressor seems like overkill for a small shop, you should have as big a compressor as you can afford. Most paint-gun manufacturers recommend a minimum of 3hp.

Jon Kosmoski of House of Kolor. Jon has painted thousands of motorcycles and won nearly that many awards for Best Paint. He feels that most first-time painters fail due to poor preparation and poor materials. In particular, Jon insists that the primer used on motorcycles be a two-part epoxy primer.

Work Area and Supplies

Like any other repair or fabrication process, painting requires a clean work environment equipped with quality tools. At the top of the list, the biggest and most obvious tool needed in even a small paint shop is the compressor.

Most paint manufacturers recommend that the shop be equipped with a compressor of at least 3hp capable of supplying 10-11cfm (cubic feet per minute) at 40-50psi. Others insist on at least 5hp. Yes, you can spray with a smaller compressor and wait occasionally for the compressor to catch up—but like everything else, there's a price to pay.

The smaller an air compressor is, the harder it works while you spray. An air compressor that is hammering along trying to keep up is more likely to pick up oil from its own crankcase, and also produces hot air, which will cool in the lines, leaving water droplets in the air stream to mar your paint job. Luckily for most of us, motorcycles are made up of a number of relatively small pieces, so the painter can take a break between the tank and fenders, for example, and let the compressor catch up. The lesson here is simple: If you don't already own or have access to a good compressor, buy the biggest one you can afford.

Keeping air and oil out of the air lines requires more than just a big air compressor. As pointed out by Jon Kosmoski, well-known painter and owner of House of Kolor, the air distribution system is just as important as the air compressor. Jon insists that the main feeder line from the compressor be galvanized pipe (copper would work well, too), and that the main feeder pipe run downhill slightly with a valve or plug at the low end for cleanout. A good air distribution system will help prevent impurities like moisture, oil and rust from entering the air stream—and contaminating an otherwise perfect paint job.

A water trap will help to keep any moisture in the system from entering the spray gun. Mount the water trap at the outlet for the air hose—where the air is cooler and the moisture is more likely to have condensed out—not right at the compressor.

The large compressor and galvanized pipe may seem like overkill for a small shop at home. Yet, it's hard to do quality work in a poorly equipped shop. Considering that the compressor air is used to carry and atomize the paint, and knowing that any impurities in that air stream have the potential to ruin the paint job, it makes good sense to do everything in your power to ensure that that air stream is free of moisture and other impurities.

Jon Kosmoski goes on to recommend that each drop or junction where a flexible hose is attached run up instead of down to inhibit the passage of moisture and impurities into the hose feeding the gun. The flexible hose itself should be of at least 5/16in ID (to prevent pressure drop) and no longer

than necessary. A long hose will leave too much of the hose on the floor, where cooler temperatures cause moisture to condense out of the air stream.

Ventilated Home Spray Booth

The ideal spray painting environment would provide good ventilation, no dust and bright, even lighting. A professional paint booth does indeed approximate those conditions and a good one costs only about $10,000.

If you don't have ten grand, don't give up. A simple, safe alternative to the professional booth can be constructed in your garage for a heck of a lot less. Start with one stall (or less) of your garage.

Ventilation can be provided by opening the door about 12in and filling the void between the bottom of the door and the floor with filter material. Jon Kosmoski recommends a product like Dustlok

Jon Kosmoski recommends that you use galvanized pipe for your air distribution system. Again, it might seem like overkill, but it is essential that you supply clean, dry air to your paint gun. Note that the T runs uphill before coming down to the water trap and regulator—so dirt and moisture are less likely to find their way into the air line. The big feeder line should have a valve for cleanout on the end farthest from the compressor.

27

SIZE OF AIR HOSE	AIR PRESSURE DROP AT SPRAY GUN				
INSIDE DIAMETER	10 Foot Length	15 Foot Length	20 Foot Length	25 Foot Length	50 Foot Length
1/4 inch	Lbs.	Lbs.	Lbs.	Lbs.	Lbs.
At 40 lbs. pressure	8	9 1/2	11	12 3/4	24
At 50 lbs. pressure	10	12	14	16	28
At 60 lbs. pressure	12 1/2	14 1/2	16 3/4	19	31
At 70 lbs. pressure	14 1/2	17	19 1/2	22 1/2	34
At 80 lbs. pressure	16 1/2	19 1/2	22 1/2	25 1/2	37
At 90 lbs. pressure	18 3/4	22	25 1/2	29	39 1/2
5/16 inch					
At 40 lbs. pressure	2 3/4	3 1/4	3 1/2	4	8 1/2
At 50 lbs. pressure	3 1/2	4	4 1/2	5	10
At 60 lbs. pressure	4 1/2	5	5 1/2	6	11 1/2
At 70 lbs. pressure	5 1/4	6	6 3/4	7 1/4	13
At 80 lbs. pressure	6 1/4	7	8	8 3/8	14 1/2
At 90 lbs. pressure	7 1/2	8 1/2	9 1/2	10 1/2	16

The inside diameter of your air hose plays an important role in the amount of air pressure delivered to your spray gun. This chart shows some basic air pressure drops for 1/4 and 3/4in ID air hoses when used at different lengths. PPG Industries, Inc.

(made by Fiberbond Air Filtration Products), a filter material about 1in thick, treated to trap dirt and dust as it moves through the filter. Dustlok and other products like it are available in rolls so you can cut off as much as you need.

Don't run the filter all the way across the door, though. Leave an opening big enough for a fan pointing out of the garage. The fan itself must be an explosion-proof model, available from an industrial supply house. These fans don't arc at the brushes and thus won't ignite the flammable fumes in the shop.

Dust control is provided by sheets of plastic tacked to the ceiling, hanging down to enclose the home spray booth. You can even roll the plastic up when you're finished and reuse the "walls." Be careful, though, because the plastic will hold the dust and if used too many times it can actually make the problem of dust control worse instead of better. Further control of those persistent little bits

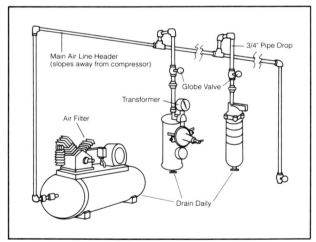

Here is an ideal setup for your air supply system. Note how the drop pipes come off the horizontal main line header from a U-shaped design; this element helps to prevent accumulated moisture at the bottom of the header lines from entering your paint gun supply hoses. To keep your air compressor mobile and to prevent compressor vibration from disrupting air line supports on the wall, use flexible air line connections between your compressor and the initial air supply riser. PPG Industries, Inc.

Most painters have a variety of guns to fit a variety of needs. The home painter can get along quite nicely with only one, but make it a good one. Illustrated are guns from Croix Air, DeVilbiss and Sharpe.

of matter can be accomplished by keeping the floor meticulously clean (use sweeping compound or a vacuum cleaner to avoid creating airborne dust) and wetting the floor down before applying any paint.

Bright, even lighting is provided by the already numerous light fixtures in your garage—right? Be careful with fluorescent lights as they don't show true color. You might have to take a piece outside to accurately gauge the new color.

Annie, Get Your Gun

Before describing the various brands of paint guns available—with the usual recommendation to "buy the best you can afford"—we have to backtrack a bit. The world of spray painting has changed in the last few years and continues to change even as we speak.

In the old days, when a Harley was either a Shovel or a Knuckle, there was only one type of paint gun. Invented by a man named DeVilbiss during the American Civil War, that early spray unit was a siphon-style gun used to spray liquid medicine. It was soon discovered that other liquids could be sprayed as well. The principle is simple: pass a stream of high-pressure air over a small siphon tube immersed in the liquid you want to spray. The high-pressure air passing over the siphon tube will pull the paint up through the tube where it mixes and is atomized by the air stream.

Like an old Harley, the siphon system is well known and dependable, though there are a few problems. In order to pull the paint up from the cup and get good atomization a relatively high pressure stream of air is needed. The high-pressure air causes the paint to leave the gun at high speed and as a result, only about half the paint actually goes on the tank or fender. The rest goes on the shop walls or up in the air.

If it were only paint evaporating into the air it might not be too bad, but the paint is mixed with a variety of solvents and reducers to make it sprayable. These solvents are known in the industry as VOCs, or volatile organic compounds. VOCs contain hydrocarbons, a major component of smog, and thus have come under strict controls in places like southern California. The California South Coast Air Quality Management District mandated Rule 1151 to reduce the estimated 38 tons of hydrocarbons that were being emitted to the air every day by the bodyshops in the southern part of the state.

High-Volume Low-Pressure Spray Guns

Rule 1151 mandates the use of HVLP spray guns to reduce the amount of VOCs sent up into the air each day; HVLP stands for High Volume Low Pressure. While the standard siphon-type gun uses a low volume of air at high pressure to atomize and carry the paint, the new guns use a large volume of

Some HVLP spray guns—these are from Croix Air—use the shop air compressor for their air supply but are supplemented by ambient air. This lowers the cubic-feet-per-minute requirement of the gun and allows the use of a smaller air compressor.

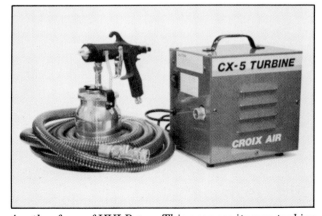

Another form of HVLP gun. This one uses its own turbine as the air supply—thereby eliminating reliance on the shop's air compressor, or questions as to its size and condition. Turbine systems also reduce moisture problems as the air is never compressed, so there is less chance that moisture will condense out of the air stream when the air cools and expands.

air at low pressure to do the same thing. Because the atomized paint leaves the new HVLP guns riding a lower pressure stream of air, there is less overspray. The industry talks of improved transfer efficiency (TE), a measure of how much of the paint actually is transferred from the gun to the object being painted.

Siphon-type guns have a rather low TE of 25 to 50 percent, meaning that half to three quarters of the paint mist fails to reach, say, the fender. What doesn't reach the fender ends up making a mess of the shop with fog and overspray, adds to air pollution and wastes expensive materials.

The new HVLP guns operating at lower pressure have transfer efficiencies as high as 95 percent! That means less crud in the air, limited opportunity for the fumes to enter your lungs, less mess in the shop and more of your expensive paint actually making it to the fender.

HVLP guns come in different styles. Some, known as turbine systems, use their own turbine, supplying a large volume of air at low pressure through a large-diameter hose. Though these systems are more expensive than a gun alone, they offer a number of advantages. Because they use their own turbine, there is no worry about the size or condition of your air compressor. The turbine doesn't actually compress the air, so there are fewer moisture problems caused by air being heated and then cooled. Gone, too, are any worries about picking up oil or other contaminants from the air compressor.

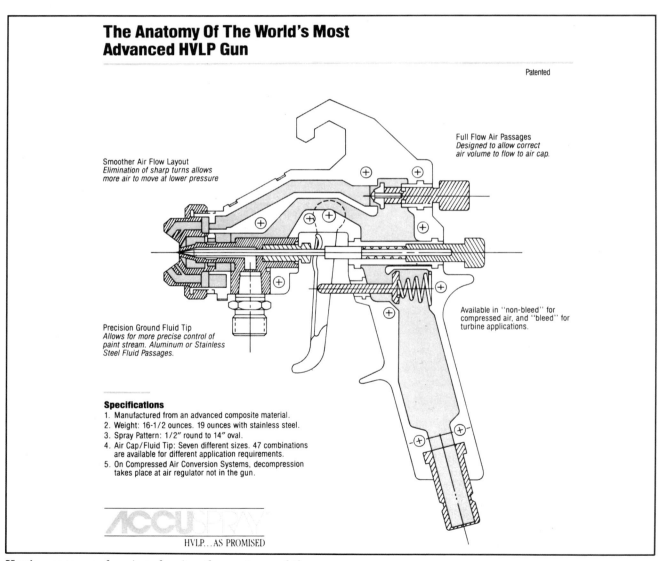

The Anatomy Of The World's Most Advanced HVLP Gun

Patented

Smoother Air Flow Layout
Elimination of sharp turns allows more air to move at lower pressure

Full Flow Air Passages
Designed to allow correct air volume to flow to air cap.

Precision Ground Fluid Tip
Allows for more precise control of paint stream. Aluminum or Stainless Steel Fluid Passages.

Available in "non-bleed" for compressed air, and "bleed" for turbine applications.

Specifications
1. Manufactured from an advanced composite material.
2. Weight: 16-1/2 ounces. 19 ounces with stainless steel.
3. Spray Pattern: 1/2" round to 14" oval.
4. Air Cap/Fluid Tip: Seven different sizes. 47 combinations are available for different application requirements.
5. On Compressed Air Conversion Systems, decompression takes place at air regulator not in the gun.

ACCUSPRAY

HVLP...AS PROMISED

Here's a cutaway drawing showing the anatomy of the Accuspray high-volume, low-pressure spray gun, available through The Eastwood Company.

More common are the HVLP guns that run off a standard air compressor. Most of these guns run on 50-80psi of air at the gun. They differ from conventional guns by their ability to convert the high-pressure, low-volume air into low-pressure air—not over 10psi at the spray head—of a higher volume. These guns are called pressure pots because they apply 2-3psi of air to the paint in the cup, thereby helping to push the paint from the pot to the air stream.

There are two styles of high-volume, low-pressure guns that run off shop air. The first type relies on the air compressor for 100 percent of its air and can have rather high air requirements. The second type passes the air through a venturi as it moves through the gun, as in a carburetor. The venturi creates a low-pressure area where ambient air from the shop is added to the air stream in the gun. By supplementing compressor air with ambient air the air requirements of the gun are reduced, meaning that the gun will run off a smaller compressor.

If you choose an HVLP gun that runs on compressor air, watch out for the compressor requirements. Some of these require a minimum of 5hp and as much as 30cfm of air at 50psi. The HVLP guns that use the venturi principle (Croix Air and some others make such models) keep compressor requirements at a reasonable level.

Before ruling out an HVLP gun as too expensive (they start at about $350), remember that you're doing more than just preventing the emission of more VOCs into the atmosphere. You will be getting significantly more of the paint (at as much as $100 per gallon) on your new bike. And a higher TE means less overspray and mist in the shop. Besides the neatness factor, that means less chance to inhale the often toxic compounds found in modern, catalyzed paints.

Whatever gun you buy, buy quality, even if you think this is your only paint job. Like hand tools, you can't do a good job with junk painting equipment. No matter what style of gun you choose, buy a brand name. Well-known companies like Binks, Sharpe, DeVilbiss, Croix Air and others make a wide range of quality spray guns and equipment.

Professionals like Jon Kosmoski and Mallard Teal have a number of guns. One for primer, one for candy, one for lacquer and a small gravity-feed gun to touch up the tight areas. But don't be fooled or intimidated into thinking you will need all those different types of guns for your home shop. Buy one gun, a good one, and keep it meticulously clean.

Now that you have your shop squared away, with a working air compressor and a good-quality spray gun, the next step is to decide what type of primer and paint to use on your motorcycle.

Primer Types and Uses

Primer paint may seem much too simple a topic to need any explanation. You just buy some, thin it and spray it—right? Wrong. Primers are available in nearly as confusing an array as final color paint coats. Primer products include metal etch, primer-surfacers, primer-sealers and sealers.

Metal Etches

An etch is used on bare metal to ensure that the first primer coat will adhere to the metal. The etch is a chemical that scours the metal surface clean.

Use of the new, two-part, epoxy primers has eliminated the need for an etch in most cases.

Primer-Surfacers

After you have sanded down the surface to be painted and perhaps used some Bondo to fill in any scratches or dents, the surface will probably still retain some small imperfections such as minute sanding scratches and uneven surfaces. Primer-surfacers are primer products with a high solids content that will cover minor flaws in the surface to be painted.

Primer-Surfacers are not body fillers, however. They are not thick enough to fill in bodywork dents and crash scratches; they are only a final finish to fill in slight sanding scratches or minor blemishes.

Primer-surfacers should be sprayed on to the surface in just light coats never more than a couple mils thick and then allowed to dry. When set up, you can wet sand the primer-surfacer for a smooth surface.

Primer-Sealers and Adhesion Promoters

Primer-sealers and adhesion promoters have the ability to seal one paint layer from another. Sealers are important if you plan on spraying a coat of new paint over an existing paint job. The sealer will protect the new paint from chemically reacting with the old—especially if they are different types of paint.

Enamel paints can be sprayed over an earlier lacquer paint job without a problem, but it is still a good idea to seal the original lacquer coat just in case. Lacquer paints, on the other hand, cannot be safely sprayed on top of enamel unless the enamel is fully cured, something that is difficult to ascertain. When spraying enamel on top of lacquer, then, you should almost always use a sealer to protect your work.

To check whether your old paint job is lacquer or enamel, you can wipe a small dab of lacquer thinner on a hidden section of paint: if the thinner dissolves the old paint, it is lacquer; if not, it is enamel.

In addition to preventing any chemical reaction between two paint layers, sealers are used to ensure good color hold out. Color hold out means that the final coats of paint will not soak into paint layers underneath, causing a dull paint job.

Epoxy Primers

Epoxy primers have come on the market recently, combining the qualities of metal etch, primer-surfacers and primer-sealers all in one product. These two-part primer products adhere so tenaciously to the metal that corrosion problems are greatly reduced.

Although they can be applied over factory primer, epoxy primers like DP 40 from PPG or EP-2 from House Of Kolor are best applied over bare, clean metal.

Wax and Grease Removers

Before your surface is ready for a primer, undercoat or top coat of color, you should always use a wax and grease remover to cleanse the surface of any traces of dirt, grease, oil, silicone or other contaminants. Oil from your fingerprints can leave a small amount of residue on a surface that will prevent paint from adhering; silicone or wax from an old wax job will do the same.

Paint Types and Uses

There are two basic types of paints used in motorcycle custom painting: lacquers and enamels, with urethane paints being a type of enamel. Within each type of paint there are several different specialty paints designed for different uses and types of finishes. The major differences between lacquers and enamels lies in their chemical make-up and how they work on your motorcycle.

Paint has three main ingredients: pigments, binders and solvents. The pigment is the base of the paint, providing the color. The binder is a catalyst that promotes adhesion to a surface. The solvent is a liquid that carries the pigment. After the paint has been shot on a surface, the solvents evaporate and the part of the paint coating left is the pigment with the binder as a hardening agent.

Enamels are based on varnish-type binders and dry in a two-step process, thus taking much longer to dry. Lacquers, on the other hand, dry quickly by evaporation of the solvent and so may be better suited to your home custom painting.

Nitrocellulose Lacquer

Once upon a time in the old days when sex was safe and motorcycles were dangerous, anyone working in a small workshop would use nitrocellulose lacquer to paint their bike. Nitrocellulose lacquer was the wonder paint of the 1930s and 1940s but with the introduction of acrylic lacquer in the late 1950s, it almost instantly went out of style.

There are two reasons why nitrocellulose lacquer went out of fashion. First, the nitrocellulose was a highly toxic additive requiring heavy-duty respira-

tion and skin protection, which was rarely used in those days.

Second, the nitrocellulose lacquer did not contain oils and could not withstand wide ranges in temperature or bumps and knocks—no matter how slight. Therefore, the lacquer needed the addition of a plasticizer to keep the coating permanently flexible. The advent of acrylic lacquer solved both of these problems.

Acrylic Lacquer

Acrylic lacquer adds the liquid plastic binder to the regular lacquer paint, providing a harder, more durable lacquer finish. Acrylic lacquer offers improved ultraviolet radiation protection, meaning the paint will fade slower than regular lacquer if left out in the sun. It also is easy to apply and dries almost instantly.

Acrylic lacquer can be applied nearly anywhere without worrying about having a paint booth to paint in.

To reach the high-gloss finish many customizers and show motorcycle painters desire, lacquer must be rubbed, buffed out and compounded to bring the shine to the forefront. Thus, lacquer requires a lot of extra work—both in application and in elbow grease later on. The end result is well worth the effort, however, and nothing matches a well-rubbed lacquer finish for depth, clarity and shine.

On the negative side, acrylic lacquer does not stand up to fuel spills and chemicals as well as the urethane paints. Cracking, often noted as a major flaw of acrylic lacquer, is usually caused by too many layers of paint rather than by the acrylic lacquer itself.

Jon Kosmoski notes that by using a two-part primer and minimizing excessive coats of paint, acrylic lacquer can still be used successfully to paint motorcycles.

A wide variety of acrylic lacquer colors are readily available.

Enamel

Enamel is less expensive to use than most of the other paints. It adheres well to most surfaces and requires minimal surface preparation. It does have its problems, however.

Enamel takes a long time to dry and so it must be applied in light coats to prevent running or sagging. The slow drying time also allows dirt, dust and insects ample time to settle.

Enamel is typically a thicker paint than lacquer, and two coats of enamel will give about the same coverage as five to six coats of lacquer. This difference in coverage is something to consider when looking at the amount of time needed in painting

How to Paint Flames

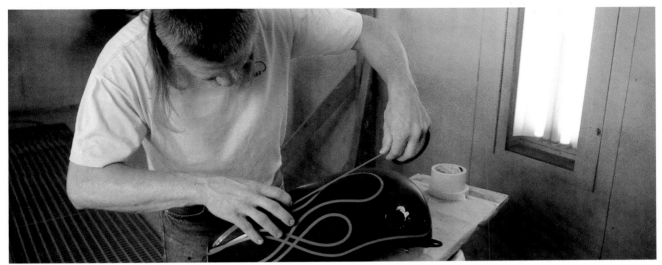

Professional bike painter Mallard Teal of St. Paul, Minnesota, starts taping out the pattern for the flames on this Fat Bob tank. Mallard tapes the flamed pattern freehand, working until he has nice licks that will look good. Then he transfers that pattern to the other side, using only his eye as a guide. The tape is 3M's Fine Line Striping tape, made of plastic and easier to bend around curves than conventional masking tape.

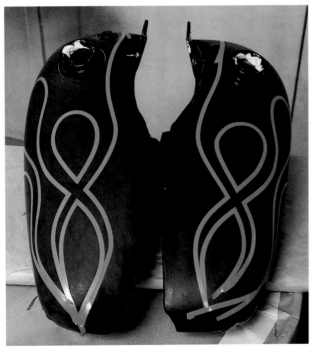

This is what the tanks look like after the initial taping is finished. The design is clean and simple, and the overlap has been cut out with a razor knife. The metal area where the gas cap seals was taped off before any of this started. The black is a urethane base coat that was wet sanded prior to the taping operation. The black will get shiny again after the whole tank is clear coated.

Mallard tapes off the rest of the gas tank using various widths of masking tape. Caution should be used to ensure that the painter's hands touch the tank as little as possible so no oils are transferred to the tank.

33

The two tanks just before the first coat of flame paint is applied. The final shape of the flames can be clearly seen here.

The tanks, after two coats of metallic silver are applied. This silver base coat is a noncatalyzed urethane. The paint and reducers used with the paints are from PPG— all are designed to work together.

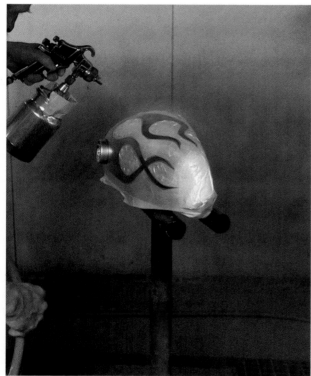

Mallard sprays the first coat of metallic silver. This is the base coat for the flames; the silver and metallic will shine through the various candy coats sprayed on later. Two light coats of the silver are sprayed, the second being applied after the first is dry to the touch. The light coats dry quickly in a downdraft paint booth with lots of air moving through.

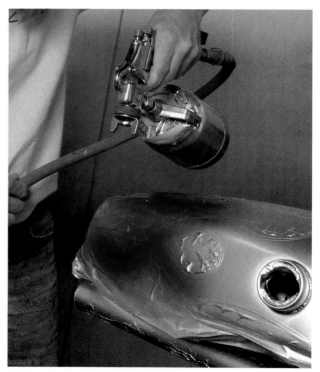

Mallard sprays the multicolored flames, starting at the back. The red tips are sprayed on first, in a candy urethane (the color is Romanesque Crimson) without any catalyst. Again, two coats are applied. A respirator was not used in order to communicate during the painting. Also, this is a downdraft paint booth, thus the volume of paint is low and the paint is noncatalyzed.

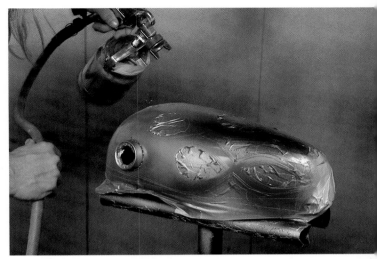

The next color in the three-part color transition is applied. This is Orange Glow, another candy color. You can see how the color blends where it meets the red tips. The tanks after two coats of Orange Glow have been applied. Once again, two coats of the candy color have been applied. Mallard has done a great job of creating the color transition from orange to red.

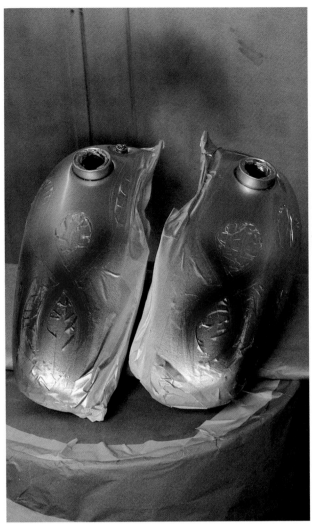

The tanks after two coats of Romanesque Crimson are applied. Paint is applied only to the tips.

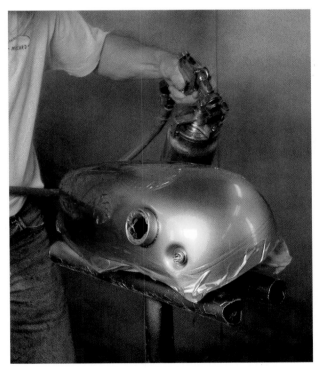

The final color is applied to the front part of the flames. This is Yellow Sunshine, another candy color. Mallard holds the air hose with his left hand, keeping it away from the gas tank and making good gun control easier. Two coats of Yellow Sunshine are applied and blended where they hit the Orange Glow. The effect of the silver metallic can be seen in the shine that comes through the Yellow Sunshine.

35

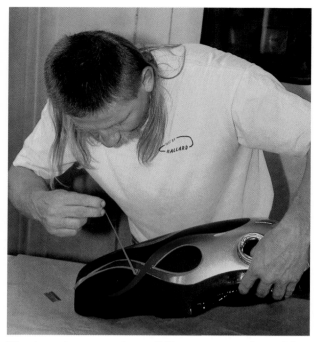

The tape is removed carefully, not more than thirty minutes after the final coat of flame paint is applied. Tape is kept at 90 degrees to the paint edge as it is pulled away. Again, caution is used to keep the hands off the paint since another coat of paint—the clear coat—still has to be applied. Very small imperfections in the paint where the flames meet the black can be corrected when the pinstripes are applied.

The finished product. The pinstriping was done in a complementary color. After striping, two clear coats were sprayed on top of both tanks. After allowing those two coats to dry overnight, the tanks were sanded with 600 grit sandpaper to eliminate any lumps or raised edges caused by the different layers of paint underneath the clear coat. After sanding the first two coats, two more coats of clear were applied so all the flame and stripe work is buried under a perfectly smooth coat of clear.

These tanks are going to look great. There is no visible line where one of the flame colors meets another. Next, the pinstripe artist will stripe the edges of the flames and then the tanks can be clear coated.

Customs Gallery

Lenny Schwartz' Sportster with the finished paint job (still missing the front fender as we go to press). This multicolored paint job was laid down over a silver metallic urethane base. Then Lenny taped off the various designs and put on the blue, magenta and teal. The colors are all candy coats that let the metallic shine through (though some additional metallic was added to the candies themselves). He credits the urethane paints for making the whole job relatively simple. They dry so fast that taped sections can be painted and the tape removed rather quickly.

This detail shot of the tank shows the complex design and intricate pinstriping. It's not too hard to believe that Lenny does this for a living. The basic design was finished and pinstriped, then three coats of urethane clear were applied. Next, Lenny taped out another set of stripes on the tank, applied some sizing and then applied Gold Leaf (this gold pinstripe is on the top of the tank and hard to see in this photo). Then the Gold Leaf had to be striped and finally—after drying overnight—the whole thing could be covered with another three coats of clear.

Here is Steve Lautug's bike in color, a Softail for the 1990s. Love it or hate it, expect to see more of these bikes as time goes by. Steve came up with the basic design and colors. Mallard Teal applied the PPG urethane Lemon Ice and Pale Orange paint.

The very nice pinstriping and lettering on this bike were done by Brian Truesdell. More than just pinstriping, the lettering and striping are a major part of the design. After the pinstriping was finished, the whole affair was clear coated for protection.

This is Ron Banks' yellow FXR with two colors of pinstriping and graphics as applied by Lenny Schwartz. This was a frame-up customizing job, and both the frame and the wheels are painted in body color. Pinstripes help to give the bike shape; without them it could be too yellow.

Jesse Johnson's bike was built at DS Specialties and painted by the infamous Mallard Teal. The base black is a PPG urethane while the flames are done in candy lacquers (don't do this at home, kids). Mallard first taped out a set of flames, sprayed a silver metallic base and covered that with a candy turquoise. After removing the tape, a second set of flames was taped out. The second set, done in Candy Grandeur Blue over a silver metallic base, partly overlaps the first set. The color of the flame licks changes as they run one over the other. The final step was two coats of clear.

Donnie Smith's new bike is nearly all hand built. The engine started life as a Shovelhead, with Evolution barrels and heads added later. The carburetor is a Dell'Orto sidedraft, the ignition is by twin magnetos. The paint is an especially wonderful creation by Kevin Winters. Using House of Kolor urethanes, Kevin painted the frame and flame licks a deep candy red, while the rest of the bike is a gold.

This shot shows details such as the open primary, the rear fender with license bracket and chain guard, and the hand-built gas tank. The unusual paint job started with a base coat of platinum pearl covered with the candy red. Then, the taping for the flames was done in reverse before spraying on the gold. After covering what would be flames with tape, a white Shimrin base was applied, followed by the gold, followed by a dusting of pearl and finally a clear coat.

Built by Donnie Smith, this Fatso was painted in some very bright, very 1990s kinds of colors by Mallard Teal. The paints are all PPG urethanes, the three colors are Hot Pink, Deep Rose and Hot Blue.

Scallops were popular in the 1950s and are making a strong comeback in the 1990s. They look good splashed across these 5gallon Harley tanks and create the impression of motion, especially the small scallops at the edge of the fender. The blue shadows and pinstriping on the tank help to give depth to the scallops.

Another Fat Boy, Tom Radd's black and white beauty. This bike is almost stock, with just a little lowering front and rear, extensions on the fenders (to visually lower the bike even farther) and the scalloped paint job.

White scallops with shadows are laid right over the black factory paint. The job was simple—the results are dramatic.

This Dave Perewitz FXR is an early model with the Shovelhead engine. The red paint was applied by Dave using House of Kolor materials. The base coat is a silver metallic, with a candy red applied next. The panel on the tank was taped off and painted with a white base coat, then with a separate light dusting of pearl. The next step was a coat of neon orange and a coat of candy red over that.

This Al Reichenbach bike looks very good in black and gold. Gold plate is used extensively, on the engine, the rims, point cover and with Gold Leaf on the tank and fairing.

A Panhead chopper from Don Hotop. The red is a candy red sprayed over a gold base by Shain Stevens using House of Kolor acrylic lacquer. The subtle flames are candy orange. Both the red and orange flames are covered in clear.

In creating this wild scalloped paint job for Willie Ditz' wild ride, Mallard Teal combined IROC teal blue (used on many late GM cars) with magenta candy pearl for the scallops.

The magenta scallops look like they were sprayed over a metallic base, but actually this is a one-step candy pearl product from PPG's Radiance II product line. The pin-striping is by Brian Truesdell.

46

Arlen Ness' ultra Fat Boy parked in the shade in Spearfish, South Dakota. Purple paint and bold, gold graphics were done by Dennis Dardanelli using House of Kolor acrylic lacquer. Candy purple was laid down over a silver base, then the graphics were added. The final touch was multiple coats of urethane clear (beginners shouldn't try using urethane clear over other types of paint).

Retro-chopper with wild flames by Arlen Ness. This multilayered paint job starts with a white pearl base, covered by fluorescent orange (acrylic lacquer) from House of Kolor.

Arlen created the wild flames by first taping off the "ghost" flames, and painting them with silver pearl. After pulling the tape and allowing the paint to dry, the ghost flames and the rest of the tank were covered in clear. Next, the second set of flames was taped off, sprayed with white pearl as a base and top coated with candy lime green. Finally, everything was buried under multiple coats of clear.

and the weight the materials will lift from your billfold.

Enamel can be sprayed over a lacquer finish without a problem, but lacquer cannot be sprayed on top of enamel as it will not adhere.

Acrylic Enamel

While many individuals continue to use acrylic lacquer to paint their bikes, more and more builders are turning to enamel products. The best known enamel product is probably acrylic enamel, used to paint everything from Ford vans to lawn furniture. Acrylic enamel is less prone to fuel problems when a hardener is used, though it dries more slowly than lacquer.

Acrylic enamel is one of the modern high-tech paints, and is also one of the most durable and weather resistant. The paint is fixed with chemicals to provide a high-gloss finish. Acrylic enamel has a much quicker drying time than enamel, and once dry, resists scratches better.

Acrylic enamel basically adds liquid plastic acrylic to the regular enamel paint as a binder instead of the standard nitrocellulose. This liquid plastic is naturally harder and more durable than the standard binder. When painting with acrylic enamel, good dust control is essential; otherwise, the paint will attract dust particles that will settle on the freshly painted finish.

Acrylic enamel is a thick, rich plant and when sprayed on a surface, it provides good coverage, tending to fill in well. A popular myth, however, is that paint fills minor imperfections on the surface. Don't believe it. Any imperfections are actually accentuated by the paint!

Most paint companies now offer a catalyzed enamel. With the addition of a chemical catalyst (sometimes called a hardener) to aid cross linking of the paint molecules, the acrylic enamel becomes more crack resistant, durable and expensive. The catalyst also adds to the gloss and chemical resistance of the enamel finish.

Acrylic enamel also resists ultraviolet radiation and is widely available in a variety of colors.

Urethane

When it comes to custom paint work, many professional motorcycle painters are excited about a new family of enamel products known as urethanes. Urethanes offer fast dry times and greater luster combined with low maintenance and super durability. Like every other great advance, the durability and gloss of the urethanes have a price.

Harley-Davidson's Factory Custom Paint Program

The folks who build Harley-Davidsons are well aware of all the custom painting being done out there in motorcycle land. Rather than have all that business go to the local body shop, Harley-Davidson has implemented two custom paint programs of its own, one for new bikes and one for used bikes.

New Bike Custom Paint Program

The custom paint program for new bikes has been cut back in recent years, and in 1992 only four custom color combinations are offered and only on FXR and Sportster models. Some of the dealers hope that the new, automated paint facility recently installed at the York, Pennsylvania, plant will mean an expanded custom paint program. Maybe 1993 will see more custom colors available on a wider variety of models.

If you want your new FXR or Sportster in a custom color, you have to order it before production for that year's bikes has started. If you waited too long before ordering your bike, you can check with dealers in your area. Many of the dealers order part of their allocation of new bikes in the custom colors.

For 1992, there are four combinations available on the new bikes:
• Peach and Birch White
• Teal Pearl and Crystal Metallic

• Platinum Silver and Magenta
• Root Beer and Tangerine

Each paint job is striped in two-color pinstripes done in complementary colors. There is no brochure available to show potential customers what the colors look like on a new bike, only a card with the paint chips. Based on the chips you will have to "imagine" what the finished bike will actually look like.

Used Bike Custom Paint Program

The used bike program is much more extensive in the variety of colors that are available. In fact, you can have your Fat Bob tanks and fenders painted in any standard Dupont color or any color available from the House of Kolor. The way the program works, you take your sheet metal to the dealer and the dealer sends it out to the painter who has been chosen in your area to participate in the paint program. The downside is time. Turnaround can be slow, especially at certain times of the year.

If your budget permits, you can order new sheet metal from the dealer, and specify that it be painted as part of the used bike custom paint program. That way you have a functional bike to ride in the meantime. You could even do this with a new bike and create a "convertible" with two sets of sheet metal and two different paint schemes.

The best place to get more information about either of these paint programs is from your local Harley-Davidson dealer.

In this case the price is both literal (urethanes cost as much as 30 percent more than a similar lacquer product) and figurative (urethanes are catalyzed with chemicals known as isocyanates). The isocyanates are sufficiently toxic as to require more than just a charcoal filter mask. Most manufacturers require the use of a fresh air mask and complete paint suit with rubber gloves when handling and painting with catalyzed urethane. Check the Safety section of this chapter and the tech sheet that comes with your paint for more on shop safety.

Urethane is an enamel by make-up, but not by the way it sprays and adheres. Because of this feature, it is ideal for undercarriages. Urethane is without a doubt the toughest finish, but also the most expensive.

When urethanes were first introduced, color availability was limited. Now, however, virtually any color is available.

R. J. from the House of Kolor models the latest in sexy painting outfits. Besides driving members of the opposite sex wild, this setup is recommended for use whenever catalyzed urethane paints are sprayed. The catalysts (known as isocyanates) are very toxic and require the fresh-air hood supplied by its own small air compressor. A charcoal-filter-type face mask should be used for all other painting operations.

Candy Paints

Candy paints are not a type of paint but rather a style of applying paint usually requiring three stages of painting. Candy paints result in a deep semitransparent finish with several dimensions of vibrant, deep, rich color.

First, custom painters shoot a base color coat on the gas tank or other surfaces; this base coat is typically of gold, silver, black or white.

Second, a top coat is applied over the base color coat. This top coat is usually a mixture of clear paint with a candy color toner. Several coats are usually applied until you achieve the color combination you desire; the more coats you add, the deeper the color hue will be. Candy color toners are available in a wide range from makers such as House of Kolor and SEM Products.

Finally, a couple coats of clear are shot on top and then wet sanded for luster.

Metallic Paints

A metallic paint is nothing more than a paint with minute metallic flakes added to the clear coat. Typically, the metallic flakes are small particles of aluminum oxide that will not rust yet sparkle and reflect light well.

Metallic flakes are available separately or you can buy metallic paints with the metal particles already mixed in. The flakes come in several colors.

Most painters shoot a color coat and then shoot the clear coat with metallic flakes on top to make the metal truly stand out. Metallic paints with the flakes mixed into the color coat have a more subdued effect. The choice is yours.

In order to keep the flakes suspended in the paint mixture, many custom painters add a couple clean ball bearings to the paint gun pot and shake the gun after each pass. If the flakes are not thoroughly suspended, you may get an uneven spread, and as the flakes are metal and heavier than the paint, they tend to sink to the bottom of the pot.

Pearl Paints

Pearl paints are similar in concept to metallic paints, adding tiny chips of a synthetic mylar plastic crystal paste to the clear coat to give a finish that is more vibrant and brighter with some of a pearl's swirl-like effects.

Follow the manufacturer's suggestions as to how much of the pearl paste you mix with your paint and shoot a sample on a practice piece before you begin painting your gas tank.

Shop Safety

The materials you will be using in your home shop are dangerous, hazardous and often toxic. We all like to think we're tough and that only wimps worry about respirators and all that silly safety stuff. The truth is that long-term exposure to the dust and chemicals of a bodyshop will ultimately impact even the biggest, toughest biker. The lungs you have today are the only ones you're ever going to get. Don't inhale dust from bodywork (it may never leave your lungs) and don't inhale paint fumes, especially those associated with catalyzed paints.

When sanding or doing any bodywork, always wear at least a good dust mask. Any type of painting requires a good face mask system with charcoal filters. The filters should be placed in an airtight chamber (like an empty coffee can) when not in use because their life span and ability to filter out chemicals is limited. Be sure the shop has adequate ventilation so fumes are cleared from the air.

As I mentioned earlier, the new urethane paints are catalyzed with compounds known as isocyanates. These are extremely toxic substances. OSHA (Occupational Safety and Health Administration) recommendations include a fresh-air system, so the painter breathes no shop air. The recommendations also include a painter's suit (like a light-duty coverall) and rubber gloves.

Finally, remember that many of the liquids used in painting are highly flammable. Use caution not only with cigarettes but also with ventilator fans, heaters and the pilot lights on the shop furnace.

Your First Paint Job

So you're ready with the shop, the gun and the paint. Before pulling the trigger, there are a few common-sense guidelines to follow.

• The paints you use—primers, sealers, top coats and clear coats—should all come from the same manufacturer. This way you will avoid problems with lifting and wrinkling often caused by the incompatibility of two paint systems with slightly different chemistry.

• Besides buying all your paint and thinners from one manufacturer, stay within one family of paint products.

• Don't apply a urethane clear coat over a lacquer base coat (even if some of the other kids are doing it), and don't apply a PPG top coat over a House of Kolor base coat.

• When you buy paint, ask for the technical information for each product. These tech sheets provide a wealth of information designed to help you mix and spray the product correctly.

Preparation: the Foundation of Your Paint Job

The work done during the preparation part of the paint job is just as important (perhaps more important) to the look of the final job as is the actual painting. Small imperfections and dings that seem almost invisible when the parts are in primer will be magnified a thousand times after the finish paint is applied.

The first step is removal of the old paint. The original paint should at least be sanded down to the factory primer coat. If there is more than one coat of paint on the bike or if you will be painting with a different type of paint than what was used the last time (like putting enamel over an old lacquer paint job, for example), you should strip the parts down to bare metal. By going all the way to bare metal you control the steps and the materials used for the paint job.

Chemical strippers have come a long way in the past few years. New stripping products are much less toxic and much easier to handle. Sandblasting is an option too, though the person operating the equipment must avoid too much pressure and heat

Many of the materials used in painting are flammable, not to mention all the other flammable substances in the typical shop. So, a good fire extinguisher is something that every shop should have. Custom Chrome

The beginning: this tank has just been primed with House of Kolor's Kwikure epoxy primer, KP-2. Epoxy primers adhere very well to the metal underneath and resist most types of corrosion and chemicals, including gasoline spills. Ideally, epoxy primers should be applied to the bare substrate, not to old paint. You can see that the area where the cap seals has been taped off and will be left bare for a good seal between tank and cap.

Before starting to paint, Don from House of Kolor tests and adjusts the pattern coming out of the spray gun. Getting a good pattern and the correct amount of material takes practice and experience.

—which will cause warpage and embrittlement of the metal. Remember, too, that silica sand has a bad habit of getting into places it isn't wanted, like your gas tank and your lungs. Carefully tape all the openings and then flush the tank after sandblasting. Because of the safety factor, be sure to wear a hood and quality filter during the sandblasting process.

Spray Gun Control

Before pulling the trigger on that first pot of primer, take a minute to understand and practice good spray gun control. First, always keep the gun perpendicular to the surface being painted. Second,

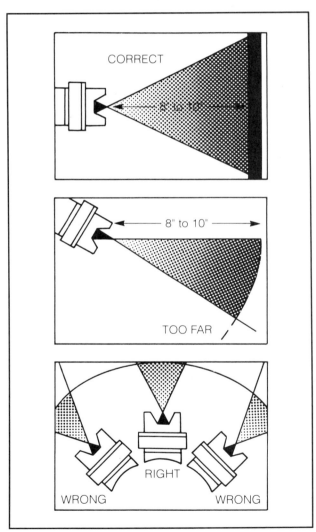

Spray gun nozzles should remain perpendicular to the surface you are spray painting. If you twist your wrist with the gun, move it too far away or simply shoot the paint at an angle, you will get paint sags, build-ups, orange-peel finishes or a host of other problems. Practice on a test panel before you begin shooting your nicely prepped Fat Boy gas tank. PPG Industries, Inc.

maintain an even gun-to-surface distance (on the order of 6-8in). Third, always keep the gun moving while spraying. There should be some overlap between one pass of the gun and another. How much depends on the material and the manufacturer's recommendations.

Good gun control comes with practice and concentration. If there's another old tank in the garage, or maybe the hood off an old Chevy, take a minute to adjust the gun and practice good, consistent control.

Applying the Primer and Sealer

The epoxy primers are especially important to motorcycle painting. When House of Kolor's Jon Kosmoski, a man who has painted thousands of motorcycles, was asked recently where first-time motorcycle painters make their mistakes, he replied: "When people paint at home, they get in trouble because of poor preparation. Sometimes they don't do enough and often they don't use the right materials. One of the biggest problems with motorcycle paint jobs is blisters around the fill caps. One problem is the lacquer primer. Even if the top coat is a urethane, the gas will seep underneath the urethane because of the lacquer primer, and cause blistering. If painters would use an epoxy primer on those gas tanks there wouldn't be any problem. Also, they shouldn't paint or prime the area where the gas cap seals—this should be left bare metal. This will provide a good seal and help to avoid blisters."

After the sealer is applied the tank appears one, uniform color. One coat of sealer is usually sufficient, never more than two, using a spray pattern overlap per the manufacturer's instructions. Most manufacturers advise application of the base coat not more than two hours after the sealer.

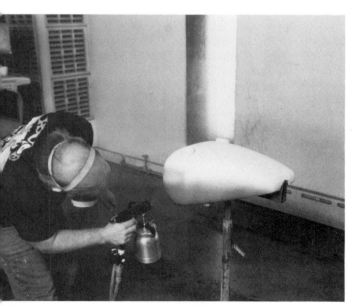

Don applies the sealer before putting on any base coat. Sealers are often used to prevent finish coats from sinking into primer—in which case the final color is affected. Sealers are available in various colors to better match the paint that will be sprayed on top.

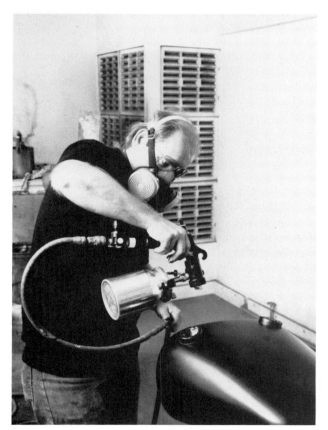

Don applies the base coat. Note that the gun is kept a uniform distance from the tank (6-8in) and that the spray head is always perpendicular to the surface. Many of the new base coats dry dull and get their shine from the candy or clear coat that is applied as the top coat.

The sparkle comes through after the application of the candy coat (spelled Kandy in Jon's product line). Base coats can be used as the final color and top coated with clear, or the color of the base coat can be altered by applying a candy on top of the base coat. The different colors, shades and effects that can be achieved are truly endless—ask for a color card to examine some of the possibilities.

This FXR carries a three-color paint job, black and white separated by an orange band. It's very tasteful and helps the bike stand out from others—yet it isn't too loud or bright.

Once you have stripped the tank, repaired any dents and applied body filler as necessary, you are ready to paint. First, be sure to mix the two-part epoxy primer thoroughly and then let it incubate per the instructions. Most manufacturers recommend the application of three wet coats, allowing flash time between each coat, and a 50 percent spray pattern overlap. If you are spraying over bodywork or trying to cover imperfections, two additional coats may be required. Epoxy primers need time to cure after the application—be sure to allow sufficient cure time before sanding.

The primer should be wet sanded with 400 or 500 grit paper before the application of more paint.

The use of a sealer between the epoxy primer and the top coats depends on the manufacturer's recommendations and your personal preference. Read the tech sheets and when in doubt, take the time to apply a sealer coat before putting on the top coats.

Always use a tack rag to wipe off any dust before applying sealer or top coats. Sealer should be applied in not more than two coats, using a 50 percent pattern overlap and allowing flash time between each coat. Top coats should be applied not more than two hours after applying the sealer for best adhesion.

Applying the Paint

Once the primer and sealer have been applied, the possibilities are nearly endless. Base coats are available in both acrylic lacquer and urethane, with and without metallic. You can use a top coat with a candy coat and then follow with a clear coat (candies are translucent paint materials that allow the color of the base coat to shine through; the final color is determined by the combination of base coat and candy coat). Pearl materials are available as well. A more subtle effect than a metallic, the pearl concentrates are usually added to a clear coat to achieve that "glow from within." Use a little imagination and yours could easily be the best-looking bike in front of the saloon next Saturday night.

Because the application, dry times between coats and sanding differ depending on whether the paint is lacquer, straight enamel or urethane, tech sheets must be your guide for specific painting applications. Most of the paint manufacturers have technical service numbers you can call and most are more than willing to answer questions (even those that might seem dumb) and help in any way they can.

When you are all done, your new paint job will be both good looking and durable. Though it might not be cheap, by doing the work in your own shop, the cost will go from out-of-sight to merely expensive. And you've got that old-fashioned satisfaction of having done it yourself.

Chapter 4

Pinstriping, Graphics, Flames and Engine Painting

A good paint job needs only a few accents to really make it stand out. A solid yellow might need blue or teal pinstripes and highlights to add a little contrast and accentuate the paint job. Pinstriping is one of those areas where you get a lot of impact from a small amount of paint.

Most riders, even those who would take on the job of painting their own bike, wouldn't attempt to do their own pinstriping. Yet, if the design is simple and the bike builder a little daring, there's no reason you can't do it yourself. The following sections will tell you how. But again, even if you don't want to attempt it, a knowledge of the tools and techniques required will make you better qualified to hire a professional pinstriper.

Required Materials

Pinstriping requires special tools and materials. At the top of the list are the artist's brushes, those funny-looking brushes with the long bristles. On a

This is what flames and pinstriping can do to your bike! This is a relatively conventional set of flames on a Dave Perewitz bike. These run yellow-orange-red on a brandy wine base and overlap just slightly. Note how well they fit and follow the custom tank. Each lick is outlined by not one, but two pinstripes. Dave did this paint job in acrylic lacquer.

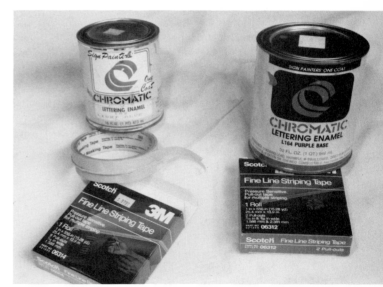

Pinstriping can be done at home, though it requires specialized materials and tools. 3M Fine Line Striping tape comes in different dimensions with different sizes of pull-outs for varying widths of lines. Chromatic is an inert sign-painting enamel designed to go on over almost any type of paint without causing a reaction. This paint comes in a large number of colors to meet most needs. Mixing can create the shades not available as mixed colors.

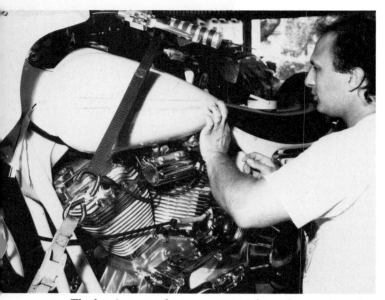

The key is to get the tape on straight and smooth, and to be sure the edges are adhering securely so no paint can creep up underneath the edge of the tape. Lenny Schwartz of Krazy Kolors recommends running your forefinger or thumb down the tape one last time just before painting.

good brush the bristles are usually made of camel or squirrel hair. The brushes are rated numerically, from 00 to 5, with 00 being the smallest and 5 the largest. To get started, you probably need two or three of the smaller-sized brushes. Professional stripers often make a 000 size by cutting half the bristles out of a 00 size brush. Buy yourself two or three small brushes from a company like Mack or Dagger, available at most art supply stores.

Next, you need some masking tape. Not just *any* masking tape, but 3M Fine Line Striping Tape. Think of it as six or eight thin strips of tape on one roll. You put it on straight and smooth, and then you pull out one or more of the small strips to leave an opening (or two) ready for paint with masking tape on either side of it. You can find 3M Fine Line tape at most automotive paint and supply stores.

Finally, you need some paint. Not just *any* paint, but paint designed especially for pinstriping. Perhaps the best known of the striping paint is 1 Shot sign-painting enamel. Designed as an inert paint, 1 Shot can be applied to nearly any other painted surface without worry that it will react to the existing paint.

Another paint choice is Chromatic lettering enamel. Also designed as an inert paint, Chromatic

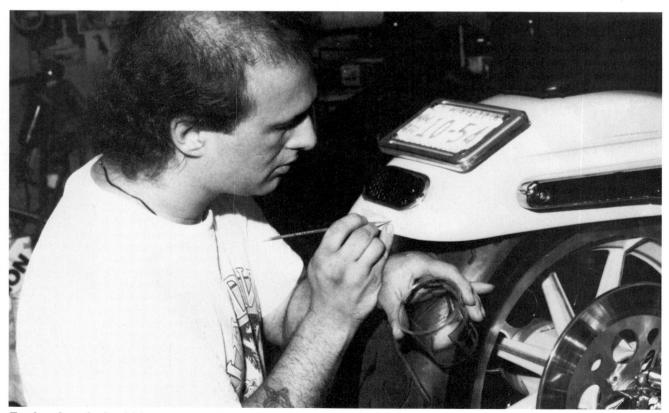

Freehand work should be avoided until you have some experience. Note that the right hand is supported and steadied by the left.

is available in a wide range of colors and can be applied over other paints.

Perhaps the most durable of the pinstriping paints is a product offered by Jon Kosmoski's House of Kolor. Their Sign and Lettering enamel is a true urethane and offers the durability that only a urethane can achieve. In addition, the House of Kolor offers a wide range of wonderfully bright colors. Unlike some other urethane base coats, these enamels dry shiny and do not require a clear coat to achieve a gloss. If, however, you are not going to clear coat the urethane stripes, the color coat itself must be catalyzed. If the stripes are going to be covered in clear, then the urethane can be applied without a catalyst.

All of these pinstriping paint products are available at your neighborhood auto paint and supply store.

Pinstriping Technique

Laying down a nice line is a special skill acquired after considerable practice. Beginners should rely mostly on the tape and limit their freehand work until they have more experience. Lenny Schwartz of Krazy Kolors in St. Paul, Minnesota, suggests that the novice striper practice on another tank or maybe that old Chevy fender until you learn how much paint to put on the brush and how to control the brush so a nice, even line is achieved.

Before applying the tape or trying to lay down a line, the surface must be clean, clean, clean. Lenny suggests using Prepsol, a solvent commonly used by painters (after a thorough wash job). Special sign-painter's Prepsol is available for problem areas as one of the biggest headaches for a striper is removing waxes and polish that contain silicones.

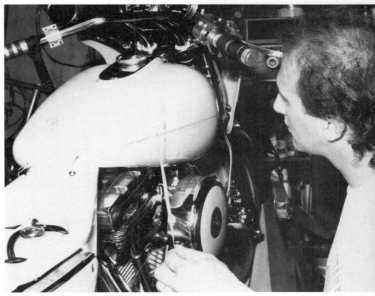

Tape should be pulled off shortly after lines are painted. If left too long, tape may pull the lines off with it. Mistakes in painting can be wiped off with a rag, or a rag dabbed in thinner if the paint has already set up.

Lenny suggests trying a little of the striping paint on a small area of the tank or fender before the actual striping begins. If the new paint "fisheyes," then more cleaning is needed. In a worst-case situation, fisheye eliminator can be added to the striping paint.

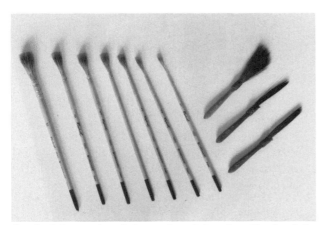

On the left, a series of sign-painter's brushes. On the right, a set of pin striping brushes with their long bristles, starting with a 0 and progressing to a 5. The good brushes are made of camel or squirrel hair and must be kept in some kind of solution between jobs. Lenny keeps his brushes in automatic transmission fluid and feels that this keeps them in optimum condition for striping.

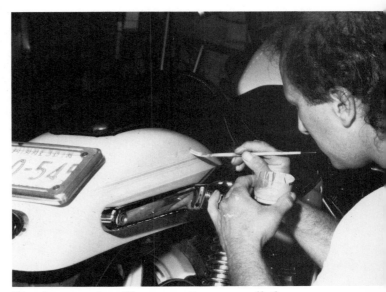

Heartbeats and oscilloscope patterns are all the rage. These are usually done freehand with a sign-painter's brush, one with relatively stiff bristles. Note again that one hand supports and steadies the other while applying the paint.

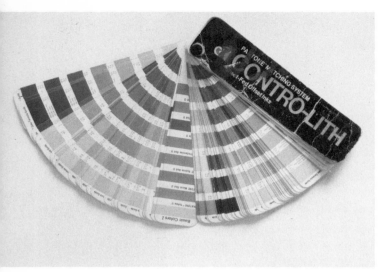

A PMS chart can be a great guide to choosing the right colors for your bike or for the pinstriping and graphics. It's easy to hold a particular color up to your current paint job to see how the two go together, or to simply hold two colors next to each other to judge the effect.

Once the surface is ultra clean, the striping tape can be laid down. Because the tape has numerous pullouts you can have one thin or a thin and a thick line, side by side. Your design will depend on the style you've chosen for the bike and your personal taste. When in doubt, remember that less is more (thin lines look more professional than fat ones). And besides, you can add to the striping later. With the multiple pullouts of the 3M tape, you can easily run two parallel lines of different colors along the contours of the fenders and gas tank.

At least half the battle of laying down a nice, consistent line is in learning how to correctly thin the paint. You need the right paint consistency. Thin it too much and the line spreads to the sides and has no definition. Thin it too little and the line is dry with bare spots where no paint was transferred from the brush to the gas tank. As a starting point, you might try one part paint to one-quarter part thinner.

Deciding which colors to use in the stripes is a tough call. You might get a color chart or PMS book to use as a guide. Available from an artists supply

Built at DS Specialties, this Softail owned by Jesse Johnson carries a wild, flamed paint job. The flames are multilayered, done in two colors of candy blue sprayed over a silver metallic base.

Details, details. Note how the flames lick around the gas cap and then across the tank—one over the other. Pinstripes really give definition to the flames.

store, the PMS book contains hundreds of color samples and the formulas for making them. Find a color you like and hold it up next to the gas tank to see how the two colors look together. Though the book and the formulas are intended for a commercial printer, you will at least get an idea how much of each basic color a particular shade contains.

You're probably thinking, "What if I make a mistake?" Mistakes, at least fresh ones, can be wiped off with a rag. Even the next day, 1 Shot or Chromatic enamel can be taken off with a dab of thinner on a rag. When using the urethanes you have to be more careful, as they adhere with more tenacity to the surface underneath. Anytime the stripes are laid down over a fresh paint job, one only a few hours old for example, the striping paint tends to stick better and quicker to the paint underneath. When stripes are laid down over a urethane paint job, the urethane should dry for two or three days or the tape may cause the fresh paint to wrinkle.

The biggest key is to lay the tape down smooth and straight, and to make sure it sticks uniformly to the tank or fenders. Lenny suggests running your thumb or forefinger down the tape just before painting a particular section to ensure that the edges are adhering securely. With plastic or fiberglass surfaces (like fairings and bags), static electricity can be a problem. The simple cure is to wipe the surface down with a damp rag prior to painting.

The keys to an attractive pinstriping job are choosing good color combinations, keeping your design simple and taking your time. This is definitely a case where haste makes waste.

Painting Your Engine

Though we always think of a motorcycle engine as being some shade of silver, perhaps polished and maybe with black cylinders, there is no reason you can't paint all or part of the engine in any shade you like. Paint the cases and cylinders to match the bike and then have the edges of the fins polished. The

Different strokes, this beautiful eagle was painted by Horst in shades of blue and lavender on a red base. The whole thing is buried under multiple coats of clear.

only area that is hard to paint is the cylinder heads, due to the heat around the exhaust port.

Like any other painting process, successfully painting the engine depends in large part on the preparation. The cylinders and cases have to be free of any oil film or road grime. Assuming the engine is disassembled at the time of painting, the parts should be thoroughly cleaned with solvent first and then bead blasted. Bead blasting will finish the cleaning process and leave a surface that the paint can stick to.

The primer should be the catalyzed type due to its increased adhesion. Use DP 40 from PPG or EP-2 from House of Kolor, or a similar product from another paint manufacturer. Finish paint should be urethane, one of the one-step catalyzed urethanes (not a two-part system requiring a clear coat). The urethane final coat will be quite durable, resisting gas and oil stains, not to mention rock chips.

There, everything you wanted to know about painting but were afraid to ask. The one essential ingredient that no one else can supply is the willingness to give it a try.

Chapter 5

Bolt-On Customizing

Most builders of Harley-Davidsons are not Arlen Ness, Donnie Smith or Dave Perewitz. Most of us are individuals of moderate skills and moderate budgets. This chapter was conceived as an idea chapter—ideas for individuals who don't plan to build a full-on custom bike.

The basic concept is simple: most of the good-looking custom bikes are really no more than a nice paint job combined in a tasteful way with some carefully chosen accessories. Because many of those accessories are chrome plated, a portion of this chapter is dedicated to explaining what it is that creates the magic sparkle of chrome, the sparkle that never seems to go out of style.

Another portion of the chapter is devoted to following trends. What are people doing with their Sportsters, FXRs, Softails and Dressers? What parts and techniques are people using to create their new bikes? The emphasis here is again on the newer models.

The discussion might be called a compendium of biased motorcycle journalism—modern custom Harleys as seen from here. This is not intended to be the definitive list of things that can or cannot be done to an FXR or Softail. This is more food for

The chrome-plating process can be broken down into three separate operations: cleaning, polishing and plating. Here, the old rocker covers are dipped into the cleaning solution. The cleaning process may differ, depending on whether the parts are greasy, painted or plated.

Built at DS Specialties in Minneapolis, Minnesota, Jesse Johnson's Softail is a more modern interpretation of an old theme. A bike that borrows from the chopper look without trying to be one. Flames, yes, but multilayered and definitely not traditional. Skirted fenders are timeless while the RevTech wheels are new and the fishtail pipes are old. High bars and tombstone taillight work well with the rest of the bike.

thought. If you disagree with the ideas and opinions presented, that's fine. Maybe they can be a starting point for your own, very different, project.

Taking the Mystery Out of Chrome Plating

Though numerous parts are available in chrome, it is often necessary to take your parts to the local chrome plating shop. Whether the intent is to re-chrome a primary cover that was originally plated —or to add extra sizzle by chrome plating a swing arm that is normally painted—you will be looking for someone to do a quality chrome plating job.

When you start looking for a good plating shop, the best recommendation is word of mouth. When you see a bike with a lot of nice chrome, ask the owner where he had it done. The best advertisement is the kind that's free.

In order to help you better understand the process of chrome plating, and the difference between good and bad plating, a pair of Harley rocker boxes were followed through the plating process from tank to tank—from old and crusty to new and shiny.

In brief, the process of chrome plating can be broken down into three major parts: striping, polishing and plating. Striping removes all dirt, grease and old chrome. Polishing gives the part that mirror-like finish. Plating adds to the shine and protects the shine from oxidation. What follows is the step-by-step process that the rocker boxes went through during their metamorphosis from scuzzy to shiny.

Striping, Cleaning and Degreasing

The shop is Ken's Metal Finishing in Minneapolis, Minnesota. Ken's does a combination of small-run production work and individual work for car and bike owners. Run by three brothers, Ken's has been chrome plating Harley parts for two generations.

At Ken's, one room is set aside for striping. The first step for our rocker boxes is the degreasing tank. After all the old grease and road grime have been removed the parts run through a water rinse. Because these rocker boxes were painted at one time, they take a dip in the aircraft paint stripper.

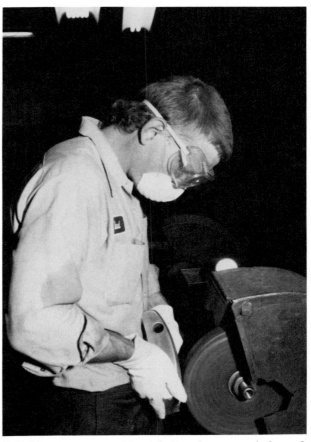

After degreasing and striping away any old paint, the rocker boxes are down to bare metal. The cleaning part of the operation is over and polishing can begin.

Polishing starts on an 80 grit belt and progresses through a number of belts and wheels from coarse grit to fine. Here, Brad uses a buffing wheel and polishing compound as he nears the end of the polishing operation.

If the parts were originally chrome plated they would be run through the deplating tank. Like the plating process in reverse, the deplating process pulls the old chrome plate off with an electrical current.

Polishing

Polishing is the foundation of a good plating job. Like the body work that is done before the paint job, polishing is the work that really determines how good these rocker boxes will look when they're finished. Scratches and pits that are left in the metal will always show through the plating. More than half the total money you spend on a chrome plate job is spent here in the polishing part of the operation.

Polishing is skilled labor. Though it may seem at first like a simple process of going from 80 grit to 800 grit, there is more to it than that. A good polisher understands the different types of metal. A good operator understands that some cast aluminum, for example, requires a deft technique or the inherent pits in the metal get bigger rather than smaller.

Though there are kits available for home polishing, this may not be a good place to trade time for money. Unless you intend to learn the polishing trade, it's usually better to let the people who do it everyday put the shine on your parts. There can be an additional problem, as most plating shops will only plate parts that have been polished in their own shop.

In the case of our aluminum rocker boxes, Brad started the polishing with an 80 grit belt, working each area until all the surfaces carried a uniform matte finish. Next, it was the 120 grit belt and then a 240 grit set-up wheel. As the rocker boxes started to pick up a little shine they were moved to an Airoflex buffing wheel with Tripolie compound for the final finish. Had the boxes been steel, the polishing steps would have been similar, although a Sisal buffing wheel and clay compound would have been used for the final finish work.

Before the actual plating of metal can begin the parts must be surgically clean. In the case of our rocker boxes they go into another cleaning tank. Then they are pulled out, scrubbed and put back in.

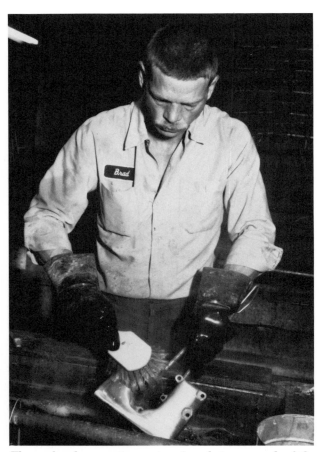

The plating process is usually made up of three separate operations, copper, nickel and chrome plating. Here, Brad inspects the rocker box after it has been in the nickel tank. Hooks at the very edge of the tank suspend the baskets of pure nickel; the bar they hang from is connected to the positive terminal of the rectifier. The rocker box itself is suspended by a copper (electricity conductor) hook from the center bar—connected to the negative terminal.

The rocker boxes get a water rinse between each of the plating operations. Besides ensuring that the rocker box is clean, this rinse minimizes contaminating the next operation with chemicals from the last. In a small plating shop the parts are handled by hand; decisions on how long and how much to plate are based on experience. Find a good shop, one with an abundance of good, cheap, word-of-mouth advertising.

Finally, a small DC current is run through the solution and the parts—first the rocker boxes are fed positive juice and then they're turned negative. The reversed polarity helps to pull off any remaining dirt or polishing compound.

Plating

The chrome plating of parts is usually a three-part process. Like a coat of primer, a thin layer of copper is usually applied first. After a water rinse, the nickel layer is applied. Finally the chrome can be put on. These three steps are where the terms "triple plate" or "three-step-plating" come from.

In the case of our aluminum rocker boxes, there is an additional step. After cleaning, the boxes are dipped briefly in a tank of nitric acid to remove any lingering oxidation. Then they are rinsed and dipped in a zinc solution. Because copper doesn't adhere well to aluminum, the thin layer of zinc will give the copper something to stick to.

The copper tank is a large metal vat filled with a liquid solution. At the edges, small baskets filled with pure copper hang just below the surface. This pure copper from the baskets is continually dissolving, leaving copper ions (charged atoms of copper) suspended in the solution. The rocker boxes are suspended from the center bar by copper hooks.

DC electricity is the force that causes the copper atoms to bond to the rocker boxes. The bar across the tank is attached to the negative terminal while the bags at the edge are connected to the positive terminal of the rectifier or DC power supply. Brad turns on the electricity and adjusts the power to about 3 volts and 70 amps. Our rocker boxes will stay in the copper solution for only about three minutes.

Only a thin layer of copper is needed as a surface for the nickel to bond to. In most cases the copper layer is only about 0.0002in thick. However, if the rocker boxes contained pits that could not be removed by polishing, the relatively soft copper could be put on a little thicker to help fill the pits and irregularities.

The next step is a dip in the nickel tank. The process is essentially the same as the copper application: DC current is used to force atoms of nickel, held in solution, to fuse with the rocker boxes. The nickel is the material you actually see when you look at a chrome-plated part. In the case of our rocker boxes, they were left in the nickel tank for almost a full hour. The meters on the side of the tank read 4 volts and 150 amps. The actual layer of nickel is between 0.003-0.005in thick.

Sometimes the nickel-plated part will emerge from the tank with a soft gray cast, rather than a bright shine. In these cases the part is nickel buffed with extremely fine polishing compound on the order of jewelers rouge to bring out a good luster.

After cleaning and polishing and three separate plating operations, the rocker boxes look great. But it wasn't easy and no, it ain't cheap.

Because the nickel is actually quite soft, another layer of a much harder material is plated over the nickel to protect it. This is the chrome, from which the whole process gets its name. The rocker boxes were placed in the chrome tank for less than a minute at 8 volts and 500 amps. The idea is a quick dip—just 0.0001-0.0002in of chrome. This layer is actually transparent. When you look at the bright shine on the newly plated rocker boxes you are looking right through the chrome. What you see is the nickel—if the preparation was good that's all

Nearly anything you can imagine can be—and probably has been—chrome plated. Whether the part is aluminum or steel or cast iron or some odd alloy, the folks at the plating shop can probably chrome plate it. So whether you're restoring an antique or building a new custom, they can help you out.

you see—just a perfectly smooth and shiny surface unbroken by any pits or scratches.

Like a paint job or engine overhaul, good chrome plating takes time and time equals money. And like painting or engine work, there is no short cut to quality.

Brass Plating, Gold Plating and Anodizing

If your taste or project is a little unusual, most chrome shops offer other plating services. Antique bikes might call for brass plating, a special project or bike might call for 24 carat gold plate.

Some plating shops also do anodizing in the color of your choice, a popular alternative for engine and chassis parts. Anodizing only works on certain metals so be sure to check with a plating shop on your particular needs.

Sportster Trends and Bolt-On Parts

Considering the vast number of Sportsters that are sold each year, it seems surprising that so few are customized. Oh, there are some older chopper-style Sportsters around with extended forks and struts where the shocks used to be, but there aren't many customized, late-model Sportsters at the bigger events. Walk the streets of Daytona or Sturgis and you can count the really nicely modified Sportys on one hand.

The reason may be that there haven't been many custom parts designed for Sportsters. Or maybe by the time a person is ready to build a really nice bike he or she has moved up to a big twin. Whatever the reason, it seems a shame as the Sportster is certainly a good-looking bike. Sportsters have a certain basic simplicity that provides a special appeal. There's nothing extra here, just an engine, gas tank

A factory photo of a pre-Evolution Sportster. They were simple bikes then, they are simple bikes now. If accesso- *ries and enhancements are carefully chosen they can add some brightness, yet leave the simple theme intact.*

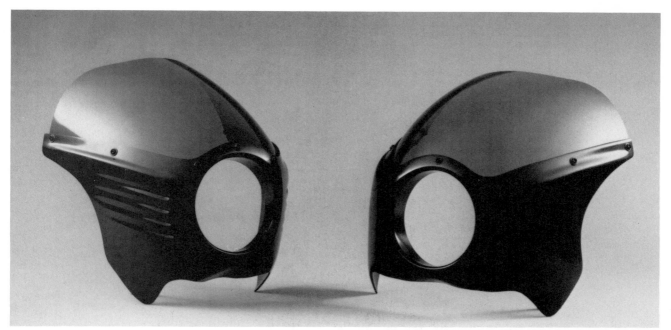

Small, Arlen Ness fairings are available for both narrow- and wide-glide front ends. These are made of ABS plastic *and have smoked plexiglass windshields. Order yours with or without louvers. Drag Specialties*

and two wheels. This is your basic motorcycle, well built and well proportioned. There's no reason this design can't be enhanced and improved upon.

Experts say the Sporty is hard to customize because there aren't many parts available, but that is starting to change. The major aftermarket

Mounted between the frame rails behind the front tire, an air dam adds a nice touch to any Harley. These air dams are all metal, crafted in a small shop in the United States.

An enterprising motorcycle builder could have one of these punched full of louvers for a real hot-rod look. Drag Specialties

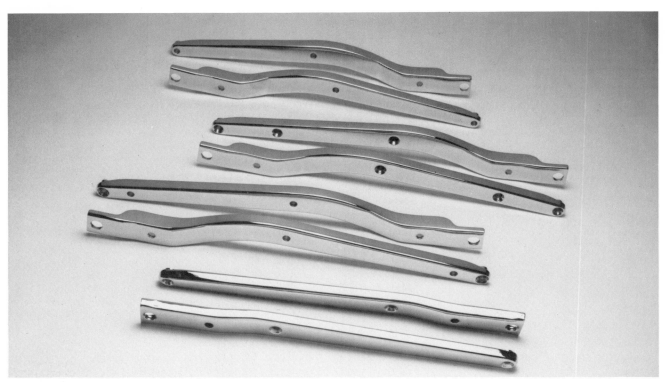

An almost infinite number of fender struts are available for most Harley models, to fit nearly any fender. You can *even buy struts with studs on the backside so no nuts or bolts show on the outside.* Custom Chrome

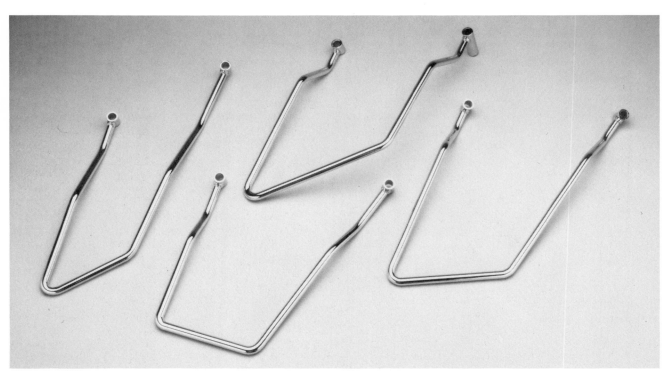

If you don't want those leather bags rubbing up against the nice paint job on your scooter, add a pair of these saddlebag supports. They are chrome plated so they don't look too dumb when you take the bags off. These will help *reduce interference between the bags and the swing arm as well, and are available for Sportsters, older FX and FL models, most Softails and most FXR model Harleys.* Custom Chrome

companies have added Sportster accessories to their catalogs in the past few years. Seats, exhaust systems, fenders and gas tanks, designed solely for the Sportster line, fill the pages of catalogs from both Drag Specialties and Custom Chrome.

Want a different look? Bolt on a Fat Bob tank, Wide Glide-style rear fender and a Corbin seat. Combine them with a nice modern paint job and some pinstriping. Because there aren't many people customizing Sportys, it's easy to have a bike that really is your very own.

The basic Sportster has changed little in appearance over the last twenty years. An enterprising rider could combine the right seat, front fender, paint job and accessories to make a late-model Sporty look like the first superbike, the legendary XLCH.

Another legendary Sportster model was the ill-fated XLCR cafe racer introduced in 1976. Ill-fated because it sold poorly when new. Times have changed and a clean XLCR is now quite collectible. The XLCR also provides food for thought if you're looking for a direction to go with a Sportster project. Duplicating the exact look of the XLCR would be tough without a gas tank, though a cafe-style late-model Sportster would be an easy thing to put together. The tail section and seat are available from Tracy. A small bikini fairing is easy to find at the local parts store or swap meet and the rest is accessories and paint to suit your tastes.

Because the Sportster is a basic design, it might be best to stay with that theme during the design and customizing of your own bike. What about a nice paint job, maybe in two tones, and a few chrome accessories. Remember that sometimes less is more. Just because no one is doing it doesn't mean it can't be done. To borrow a line from *Hot Rod* magazine: "Dare to be Different." Customize a Sportster.

FXR Trends and Bolt-On Parts

Originally known as Super Glide II, the FXR Series Harley-Davidsons were introduced late in 1981. Though the lines seem at first to be similar to

The billet aluminum look has extended to handgrips. These billet grips are knurled on each end—the throttle side comes with dual cable throttle sleeve. The left grip *has a screw-off end cap so you can keep your vehicle registration—or whatever—hidden in the little secret compartment.* Drag Specialties

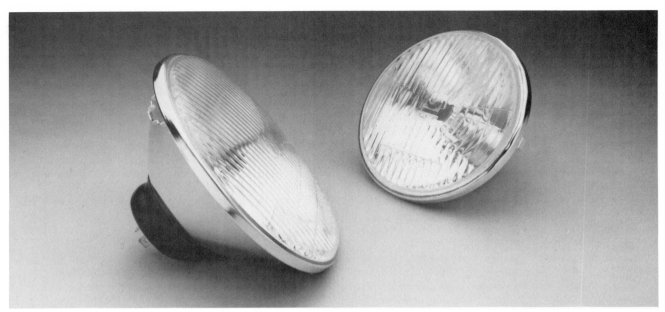

It's great to be seen, and it's also nice to see—especially at night. If you don't have a halogen bulb in your scooter yet, buy one. The difference in light when compared to the old nonhalogen bulbs is remarkable and especially critical for vehicles that have only one light. These headlights carry the standard 55/60 watt (low and high beam) halogen bulb, though high-powered 55/100 watt units are available. Custom Chrome

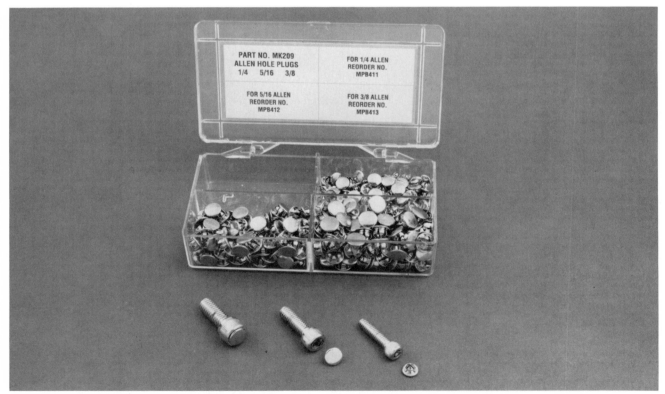

Chrome Allen bolts are all the rage for assembling a Harley-Davidson. They impart a certain high-tech and sanitary look to anything they touch. Yet, the little sockets collect dirt and moisture and, worst of all, they sometimes rust! Eliminate the problem with these nifty little end caps for Allen bolts. They help keep dirt and water out, hide any rust (rust is the pits!) and make the bolts look more like a chrome rivet. Yes, these are hot stuff. Drag Specialties

The ultimate in a bolt-on FXR. This example was built in the shop of Arlen and Cory Ness. This FXR carries all the tricks: polished lower fork legs, four-piston Performance Machine calipers on both sides with large-diameter floating rotors, Ness twin-rail swing arm, Ness fenders and fairing and of course, a fully polished engine. Note that the scalloped paint job with its horizontal lines helps to make the bike flow.

Looking like an FXR in drag, this Bob Walters-built bike goes to show that a Sportster can be the starting point for a very nice motorcycle. The small fairing, taillight-style rear fender and trim, and narrow tank give this bike a long, slim profile.

those of the earlier FX Super Glides, the FXR is a completely different motorcycle.

The frame, for example, was designed with the aid of a computer to be five times stiffer than the old FX or Super Glide frame. The steering head is well supported, and the triangular section under the seat adds enormously to the structural integrity of the frame. Instead of bolting the engine

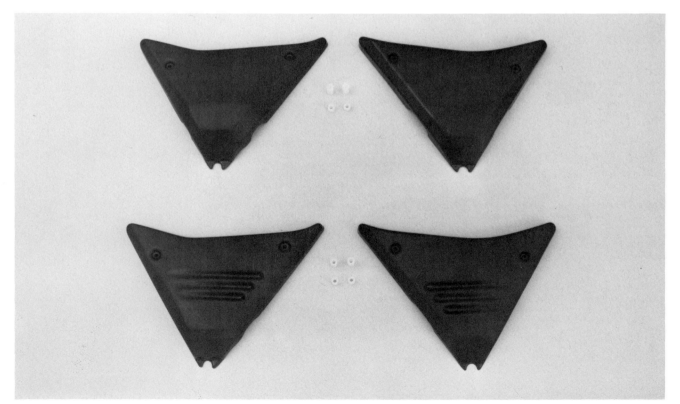

These Ness-Tech side covers are available to fit FXR models and completely cover the triangular area under the seat. They are made from ABS plastic, and are available with or without louvers. Drag Specialties

This original-style taillight will replace the stock unit or mount to many aftermarket fenders. With a chrome housing and license plate light, this taillight is designed to have the license plate mounted above it (separate bracket available). Chrome visors are also available for these lights. Custom Chrome

Clean up the looks of your Harley with this transmission and oil pump cover. Chrome plated (what else?), the covers are available in plain and louvered versions. Custom Chrome

Dress up the front of your Harley with these old-fashioned clearance lights. Added to your front fender, they add a touch of class and extra brightness—day or night. The lens is amber, the housing is chrome and the look is great. Drag Specialties

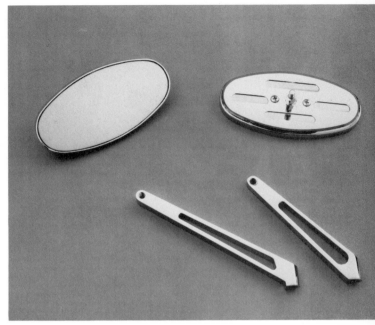

These new mirrors are part of the Stealth series accessories from Arlen Ness, and match the brake and clutch levers. Drag Specialties

directly into the frame, it was (and still is) supported by a three-point suspension system ("rubber mounted"). Instead of a four-speed, the new bike came with a five-speed transmission. Though the first bikes were equipped with the Shovelhead

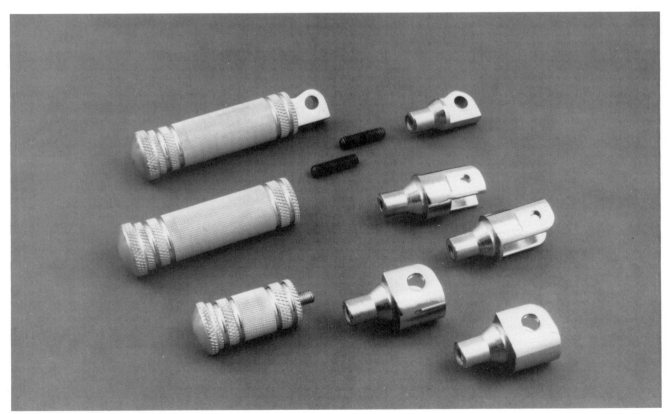

These shift and foot pegs feature the billet look and match some of the new-tech handgrips that are on the market. Drag Specialties

Steve Lautug's Softail in the foreground got the 1950s treatment, with a peach and yellow paint job, fishtail pipes—one on each side—and whitewall tires. Behind it is a similar bike, though it differs in detail (like the pink with sky blue paint job). Steve's bike carries Harley-Davidson Classic tires, while the bike behind it has tires from Cocker Tire with a slightly wider whitewall.

engine, by 1984 all FXR Harley-Davidsons were equipped with the Evolution engine.

The new frame allowed the engineers to move the battery and oil tank inside the frame, inside the triangular area under the seat. With some of the accessories hidden in the frame the bike seemed much more streamlined than the older FX bikes. The wheel base on the FXR, at 64.7in, is just more than 2in longer than the 62.3in wheelbase of the early Super Glides. The combination of a longer frame and tucked-in oil tank and battery gives the FXR a smoother look than the older FX.

This Heritage Softail benefits from the fringed look. Fringed bags and clutch and brake lever covers add a touch of elegance. Would a fringed seat be too much?

Well-known bike builder Dave Perewitz commented that when you strip an FXR they get long and low—when you strip an older Super Glide or FX, they get short and squat. The FXR lends itself to the long, low look. Riders who install flatter bars, rid the bike of the console on the gas tank and put on a small seat with no sissy bar will discover that their bike has grown, visually, into a much longer, lower motorcycle.

The long, low look can be enhanced by lowering the bike and kicking the fork out slightly. Clever designers have moved the rear fender, either aftermarket or stock, forward so it fits the radius of the tire better. If the stock rear fender is used, it can be bobbed or trimmed of the last 4-6in of metal. Visual length can be added with the right graphics or pinstriping—designs that run the length of the bike. With or without a small Arlen Ness fairing, the bikes take on a racey look, almost as if you're moving while standing still.

Softail Trends and Bolt-On Parts

Perhaps the single best marketing move made by Harley-Davidson in the past ten years was the introduction in 1984 of the Softail. With a triangulated swing arm and the spring-shocks mounted under the transmission, the whole affair was designed to look like the old hardtail Harleys. The Softail gave Harley-Davidson sales a jump start and created a lot of work for the customizing shops as well. Introduced as an extension of the then-current Wide Glide, the Softail was built as a factory custom. With Fat Bob tanks, a long, Wide Glide fork and a variety of accessories, the Softail started life as a factory-custom.

Though all Harleys seem destined for modification and personalization by their owners, the Softail seems especially well suited to men and women who want to build a motorcycle of their very own. With an engine solidly bolted into the frame and limited suspension movement, the Softail is perhaps not the road bike the FXR might be. But when a bike looks this good, who cares?

When the Softail was introduced there were only two models. Today the Softail frame is the basis for at least four separate families of motorcycles. The popularity of the machine and the tendency of Softail owners to personalize their machines means that the catalogs from the major aftermarket companies are filled with accessories for the Softail. Trying to make sense of all the modifications possible to all these bikes is a tall order, but here goes.

Starting with the frame, the Softail is unique and the aftermarket companies have designed a variety of covers and accent panels. In particular, the vertical, cast frame section behind the transmission can be completely covered in chrome or simply accented with small chrome plates that glue

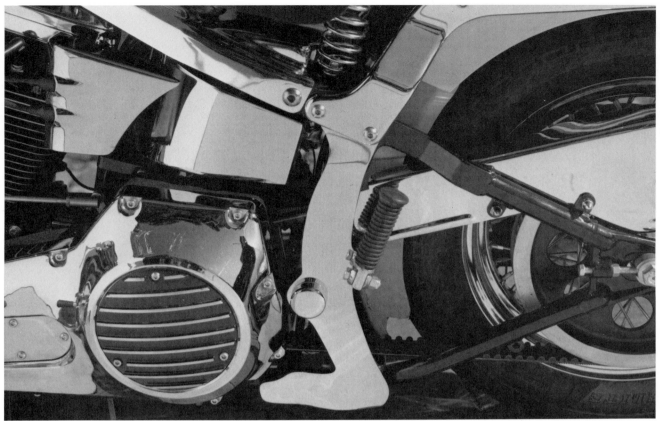

The heavy, cast frame section under the seat of the Softail series bikes can be covered with these chrome plates. They add a lot of brilliance to the bike and hide those big, rough frame sections. The swing-arm pivot bolt is covered as well by the small, round cap. Custom Chrome

Exhaust pipes affect both the looks and the performance of your motorcycle. Avoid the temptation to consider only the looks when choosing a set of pipes. These baloney-cut monsters on Bo's monochromatic Softail give it a unique look. Note the dual rear calipers and subtle signal lights.

Another option in exhaust systems. These fishtail pipes add a certain flair and create a nostalgic look as well.

Don Hotop built this Panhead with the chopper look. He took all the right ingredients—high bars, springer fork, fishtail pipes and tall, twenty-one-inch front tire—and mixed them with large doses of TLC. A good approximation of this bike could be built using a springer Softail as the starting point.

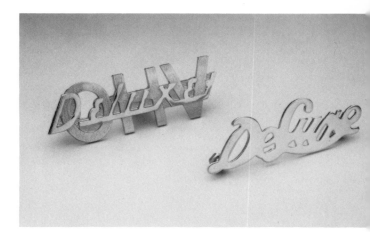

Whether you're restoring an old Glider or trying to make a Softail look genuinely old, these fender emblems from the late 1940s will lock in the correct look. They bolt easily to fenders or even leather bags with the studs on the backside. Custom Chrome

into the concave sections. A small company called KuryAkyn makes nice little chrome covers for the end of the swing arm. These little numbers hide those unsightly axle nuts and allow the swing arm to come together in a nice, chrome accent.

If your goal is simply a more sanitary Softail, add a new streamlined rear fender (with subtle skirting on the side) mounted with new chrome fender rails that allow the fender to sit closer to the tire than the stock fender. Now you probably need a new seat because of the lower fender height. Add a matching front fender, or one that works with the style of the rear fender and paint to your taste.

Arlen Ness offers a complete, chrome swing arm for the Softail, made from chrome-moly tubing.

This solo-style seat is designed to provide the look of a solo seat and separate pillion in a one-piece design. Made to fit Softails, this fringed seat is available in leather or naugahyde, black or white, with or without stitches—any way you want it, in other words. Drag Specialties

This Ness headlight is long and sleek and makes the others look positively pedestrian by comparison. With a bottom mount, this headlight fits many Wide Glides and Softails (including springer Softails) and of course, most custom applications. Drag Specialties

Featuring adjustable suspension height, the new swing arm can be used to drop the back of the bike up to 2in. And if you want a Softail with a rubber-mounted engine, Arlen can arrange that too with his new rubber-mount frame.

In more general terms, the Softail with its old-new look lends itself well to anyone interested in a nostalgia or fifties theme. Painted in peach with yellow panels for example (this paint scheme may look better than it sounds) the bike takes viewers back to the days of Ike, the days when your motorcycle was either American or English.

A few accents can really complete the nostalgia theme: fishtail exhaust, a police-style solo seat and an older Harley-Davidson logo on the tank. The whole thing can be done quite easily. The key is again the paint job and good follow through on the accessories. You can take the low-buck approach and leave the frame black—most people won't notice. What they will notice are the bright fifties paint hues and the well-chosen chrome accents.

The Softail also lends itself to a different type of nostalgia bike, the Softail chopper. The bike al-ready has the rigid-look frame. Match that to a springer front fork, skip the front fender and add ape-hanger handle bars. Mount a pair of smaller, 3½ gallon Fat Bob tanks, a solo seat and some shotgun or upswept pipes. At the rear the chopper bike would need a taildragger fender (from the Ness catalog, for example) mounted nice and low to the tire to enhance the rigid-frame look. Details might include fender rails painted body color to keep them inconspicuous and maybe some traditional, three-color, flames painted across the Fat Bob tanks.

Fatboy Trends and Bolt-On Parts

Fatboys, another permutation on the Softail theme, seem to be taking on a life of their own. Though some of the traditionalists were slow to accept the Fatboy when it was introduced, the model is currently a solid part of the Harley-Davidson model lineup.

With a relatively large area for paint, there is plenty of room to make a statement or stand out from the crowd. Paint the bike in contrasting colors

If you like floorboards but can't get them mounted where you want them, this kit may be just the ticket. They're designed to allow 7in of front-to-rear movement as well as height and angle adjustment, and can be ordered with *two different styles of floorboards. Fits most Wide Glides, many Softails and many custom applications.* **Custom Chrome**

or a bright hue and it will stop traffic on main street when you ride by. How much attention do you want?

The fat look seems to be in style, and designers and aftermarket companies are offering fenders and accessories designed to make the bike even fatter. Some of the new fat fenders are much longer than stock and come closer to the ground. It's another of those visual tricks: when the tip of the fender is closer to the ground the bike appears lower, though it rides on stock suspension. Long pipes running close to the ground have the same visual effect.

Fertile ground for customizing, a beautiful and unusual Fat Boy can be had for the price of a paint job. The accessories you add if well chosen will just be icing on the cake.

Dresser Trends and Bolt-On Parts

There seem to be more and more Dressers on the streets each year. Maybe it's the baby boomers getting older and going slower with more comfort. Maybe the FL family of bikes is finally getting the recognition it deserves as the classic American road bike. The Fat Bob tank, the big fenders, the massive fork and headlight assembly—this is it, this is what an American motorcycle is supposed to look like.

Deciding how to customize your Dresser depends on how dressed it is. If you like your FLH relatively undressed without permanent bags and fairing, it seems best to stay with the classic theme. That is, leave the bike mostly alone and don't mess with a good thing. Mount the old-style windshield if you don't like bugs, and put on a nice paint job accented

Looking old is suddenly new. This Softail features a nifty-fifties paint scheme and a good sampling of the accessories that are available to make your new Softail look old: The headlight and spotlights carry visors, the fender *carries an old-style clearance light, the horn is a replica of those used years ago and the whitewall tires really do the job.* Custom Chrome

with nice, chrome pipes that reach all the way to the back fender. If the paint is subtle, your FLH may not stop traffic—but it will be a great-looking bike. If you need more attention, do it with the paint job.

If more flash is your style, choose a brighter paint job and more dazzle in the form of chrome accessories. To say the aftermarket companies have a full range of accessories to dress your Dresser is an understatement. From chrome fender guards to chrome rotor covers, choice of accessories is limited only by your budget and taste.

Because the FLH is an older design, the bikes take well to the nostalgia treatment. Choose paint colors from the 1950s and some of the nostalgia accessories from any of the aftermarket catalogs and presto, you've run the clock backwards. Need more glitter, try more subtle accents like chrome tips on the lower lip of the front fender and rails for both front and back fenders. Ape-hanger bars are coming back in a big way and seem to look just right on an older FLH. Dual shotgun pipes or maybe fishtail pipes look like they were born on the FLH. There is fertile and perhaps unrealized ground here for some really outstanding motorcycles.

Dressers with bags (already dressed, if you will) seem to call for more of the same. Light bars, illuminated mudflaps, an illuminated cover over the front rotor, chrome rails for the bags, crash bars—where do you stop? The fringed look provides Dresser owners another way to go. The look has always been popular though it really caught on big just a few years ago and shows no sign of falling off in popularity. Fringed leather bags or fringed trim for hard bags looks right at home on a nice FLH or Ultra. Add a fringed seat and fringed covers for the brake and clutch handles. Top it off when

Rear view. More new accessories with the nostalgia look: a visor for the taillight, a wide belt cover, a dual exhaust and a solo seat with pillion pad. Custom Chrome

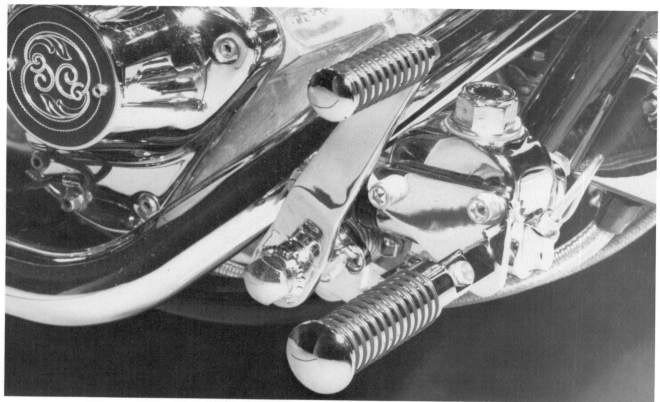

Forward controls seem to get more and more popular. This set features O-ring pegs, chrome hardware and a built-in brake-pedal return spring. Available to fit many big twin models. Drag Specialties

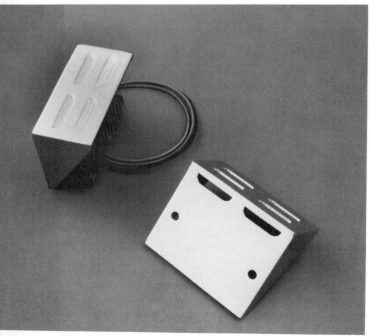

The little visor is designed to cover and brighten the voltage regulator on most Softail models. Functional louvers ensure sufficient airflow to keep the regulator cool. Drag Specialties

Check out the wild air scoop on this chopper. The automotive-style air cleaner becomes a large part of the look of this motorcycle.

A stock Fat Boy is a great starting point for a personalized Harley-Davidson. This bike belongs to Stan Fox and is the starting point for the very unique ultra Fat Boy built by Donnie Smith.

Manny's bike leaves the basics of a good design intact, adding only enough to the Shovelhead FL to bring it into the 1990s. Two-tone paint—white and light green—with matching seat and graphics across the tank add a modern accent to a classic look.

you wear one of the lovely, fringed jackets from Harley-Davidson.

Painting a Dresser is more work and money than an FXR or Softail. Besides, the paint on the late-model Harleys is very nice. If you want yours to stand out, talk to a good pinstriper. With good factory paint as a base and a lot of surface area to work on a good pinstripe artist can transform your motorcycle. A nice stripe job will help yours be an outstanding bike, one that stands out from the others in the crowd.

FX Shovelhead Trends and Bolt-On Parts

What can a person say about customizing the older FX four-speed Shovelheads. It seems everything has already been done, from chopper-style bikes to Pro-Street, race-oriented machines. Even the factory has worked a thousand variations on these bikes.

This is the after shot. Hard to believe there's any connection between the two bikes, isn't it? Despite the radical styling of this bike, most of the parts came off the shelf or out of the catalog.

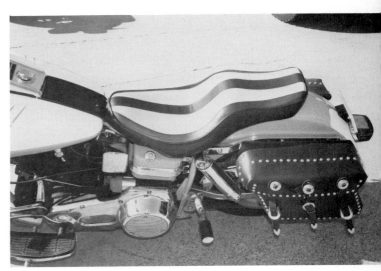

A detail shot of the FL. The striped seat adds a nice touch. Leather bags with buckles and snaps look right at home here.

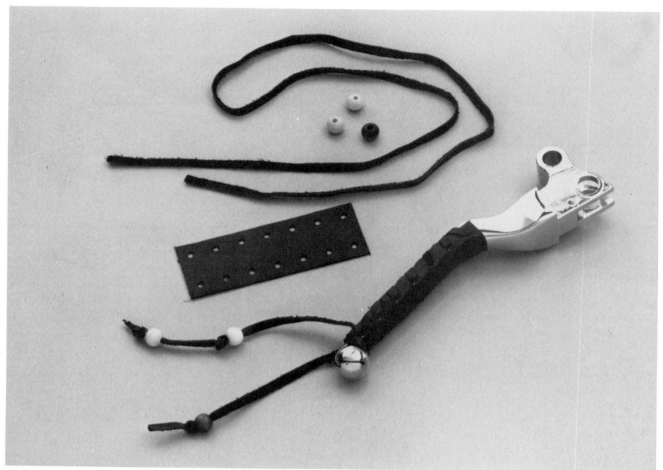

Complete the leather fringe look with a pair of leather "skins" for the clutch and brake levers. These leather covers come in black or white and have plenty of extra lacing to blow in the breeze. Drag Specialties

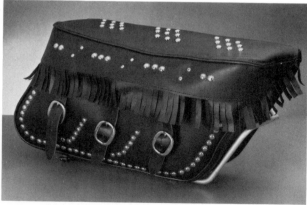

Designed to give that back-to-the-fifties look to your FLH, these king-size leather bags mount to stock saddlebag holders and utilize wire frames to maintain their shape. With more capacity than the fiberglass bags, these replacements are available in either real leather or real vinyl. The fringes and buckles theme would work in harmony with a variety of factory and aftermarket seats. Drag Specialties

What some builders are doing to the FX bikes is smoothing them out and making them look more contemporary. Starting at the rear, the fenders are supported by smooth-sided fender struts with the studs sticking out the inside (watch for tire clearance problems) combined with a small tail light assembly. Professional builders are taking this one step further by actually molding the fender rails into the fenders to create a one-piece unit. Some fenders have enough room between the tire and fender to mount the light assembly behind the fender, with only the lens showing to the rear.

Inside the fender a 130/90 or 140/90x16 tire fills the cavity and gives the bikes a nice business-like look. Farther forward, the engine can be painted body color with chrome accents. The choice of a seat is a matter of taste, though something simple without any backrest seems to best fit the theme and keep the smooth look. Keeping with the modern, slick theme, the front forks are usually Narrow Glide, perhaps shortened 2in, sometimes raked and with dual disc brakes.

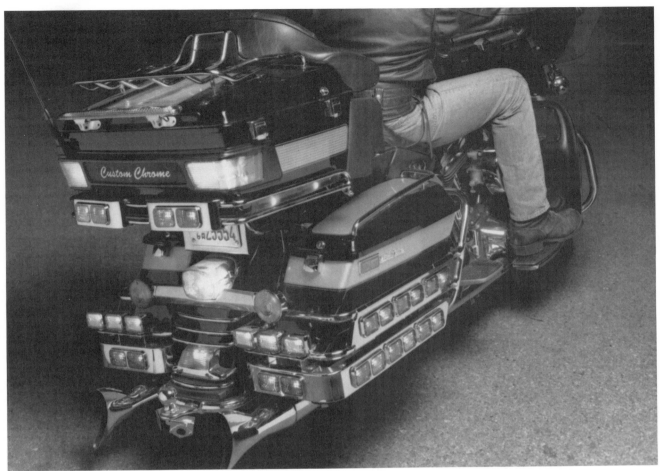

There's nothing like a Dresser at night with about a million lights. These deluxe light bar kits and panels will make your Dresser look like a Christmas tree coming down the road. Custom Chrome

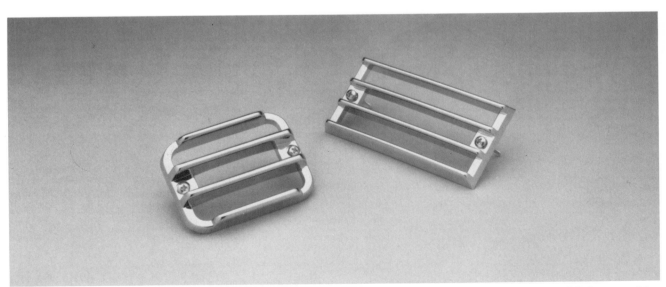

Add a little more glitter to the lights on that light bar with grilles for each lens. Available to fit the Baron lights used on TourEase light bars and also for lights from Peterson, these grilles will protect the lenses in addition to making them look more finished. Custom Chrome

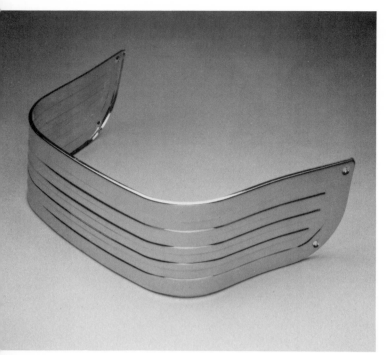

A modern FX Shovelhead by Donnie Smith. This one carries a cafe fairing, small front fender and dual disc brakes. In the rear, the fender rails and taillight are molded into the fender.

Those big FL fenders look great with this wraparound chrome trim. The trim piece is a reproduction of the factory part used on most FL models from 1968 to 1975, and will fit most Dresser fenders from 1949 through 1986. Custom Chrome

With or without a fairing, using wheels and fenders to taste, an unusual and modern Shovelhead Harley is well within the realm of reality. Look at what the other kids are doing, decide on a theme of your own and stick with your plan.

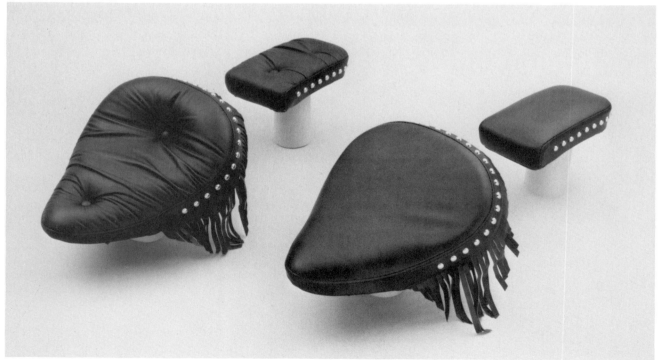

Seats come in a vast array of shapes and styles. These springless solo seats are from LePera. Available to fit a variety of FX and FL models, these seats come in leather or Naugahyde, with or without the pillion pad. Drag Specialties

New accessories are always coming on the market. This Arlen Ness bike carries a cat's-eye taillight lens and an air cleaner designed with a similar pattern.

The sleek, modern look is captured in this Arlen Ness front fender. Made from ABS plastic, this abbreviated fender fits most Narrow Glide forks right up through current models. They look good mounted close to the tire, but remember that the tire grows in diameter as speed increases. Drag Specialties

It's the little things that count—like this coil cover from Arlen designed to match the cat's-eye taillight.

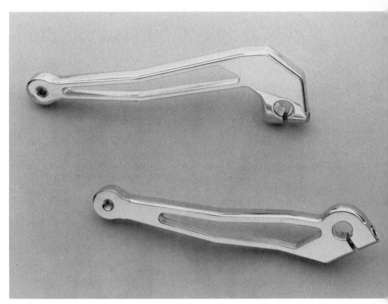

Part of the Stealth series of accessories developed by Arlen Ness. These Stealth brake and clutch handles are very contemporary. They work well with other parts in the series and fit most FX model Harley-Davidsons. Drag Specialties

Chapter 6

Modifying the Frame, Forks and Suspension

Chapter 1 suggested that you spend considerable time thinking about and planning your bike-building project before turning a wrench. Each builder has different goals, skills and finances. For some, the new bike will be a mostly stock FXR with some nice pinstriping and a few chrome goodies from the local Harley-Davidson shop. Others will settle for nothing less than a radical bike, long and low with a stroker motor and wild paint applied by the best-known custom painter in your area.

Customizers who want a mostly stock ride will probably choose to leave the motor in the frame—and the frame stock. On the other hand, men and women with the money, skills and inclination to build a radical bike will want to disassemble the bike right down to the bare frame.

Once the frame is bare, a whole new series of possible improvements and modifications become possible—once again depending on what kind of bike you really want. Tearing it down to the bare

Softail rear suspension in a bare frame. These shock-spring units pull rather than push to hold the bike up. The pivot point for the swing arm is seen just above the *shocks. Lengthening the rod on the end of the shock will result in a lower motorcycle. Some shops lower the bike by altering the bracket the shocks bolt onto.*

frame is a heck of a lot more work, but it also makes possible a host of modifications and improvements not available to builders who don't go that far. With a bare frame sitting in your shop you can clean, repaint, mold and modify it to your heart's content.

Painting and Molding the Frame

Unless the bike is new, the first modification you should make to the frame is a fresh paint job. Black is not the only color choice, by the way. And if the frame isn't black, then the rest of the bike doesn't have to be painted a color that will work with a black frame. The decision to paint the frame will open up a whole new range of paint schemes and colors.

Before you paint the frame, or have it painted, you might consider smoothing out those ugly factory welds—at least the most obvious ones near the steering head and on the sides of the frame. If your wallet is fat, then you need only tell the person painting the frame to knock the lumps off the welds and add a little filler. On the other hand, if your wallet is a little thin, you will want to spend a little time with a grinder and a bucket of Bondo. Some of the areas are hard to get at, requiring a small grinder, a lot of handwork and a great deal of patience.

Some builders go one step further, by actually adding metal to the welded frame joints and then creating a nice, smooth-radiused corner where the two tubes meet. For example, on FXR frames the triangular-shaped area under the seat sometimes needs extra attention. By carefully filling in the joints where the tubes meet with extra metal, a nice smooth curve can be formed. At least one builder took the time to match the radius of that corner frame joint to the shape of the Arlen Ness side covers. It's detail work like this that separates one really nice bike from all the rest.

Modifying the Frame

A discussion of frame modifications must begin with a short disclaimer. Not so much because of all the lawyers out there, but because the frame is the foundation of your motorcycle. Like the foundation for your house, it is the one thing everything else is built upon. Tampering with the stock frame dimen-

This Arlen Ness Softail features a—you guessed it—Arlen Ness swing arm built from chromemoly tubing with a provision for adjusting the ride height.

sions opens the door to disaster. If the work is sloppy or if the dimensions and angles are poorly thought out, you may never get to build another Harley.

Consider any frame work with caution: Use only the most experienced and respected professionals for any actual modifications or welding. And make conservative rather than radical changes to factory dimensions and angles.

Most builders and customizers who alter the frame do so to get "the look." Achieving the look usually means building a motorcycle that is lower

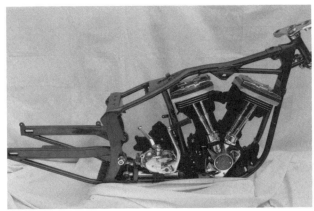

The bare frame of the pro-street bike built by Donnie Smith for Willie Ditz. The custom swing arm is based on the factory component, with the upper part of the triangle trimmed, and extended an extra four inches. The longer swing arm was fabricated as part of the Pro-Street theme. Under the four-speed transmission are special Fournales shocks with adjustments for both ride height and ride.

These kits from White Brothers are designed to lower the rear of your Softail, either early or late-model. White Brothers

The Softail frame is similar to the older FX frame, with the rear section much modified to accept the unusual rear suspension. The triangulated swing arm pivots at the large boss halfway up the vertical frame member. Shock-spring units are under the transmission, of course. The downside to this clever design is the limited wheel travel it affords.

An FXR frame in the midst of getting raked with an extra half inch of metal. That gives a final fork angle of about 37 or 38 degrees—about 5 degrees more than stock. Note that the top of the frame is not cut through and acts as a hinge.

The FXR frame after the welding has been finished. With a nice weld like this, all it takes is a touch from the grinder and some black paint to finish a quality job. Any frame modifications and welding must be done by experienced shops using highly skilled welders.

A swing arm that could only come from a Softail. Designed to look like the rear frame section from an old hardtail, this swing arm has the pivot point located above the bracket where the shocks attach.

and longer than stock. Before dropping and stretching your scooter, remember that for every gain there is a loss. A lower bike will drag more easily on corners and rough roads. A fork that has been kicked out with a 40 degree rake might look great, but it will be heavy to turn in low-speed riding. Remember, too, that part of the look can be achieved with visual cues as described in the planning and painting chapters.

Slam It!

Getting your Harley-Davidson in the weeds can be done in a number of ways. First, you have to decide how much is enough. Staying within the conservative theory advanced earlier, a drop of 1-3in seems a good compromise between form and function.

At the back of the bike, the process is fairly simple and is usually accomplished by installing shorter shock absorbers. Your local Harley dealer or independent shop can sell you rear shocks for non-Softail Harleys that are 1, 2 or 3in shorter

Like having your cake and eating it too. This Don Hotop-built Sportster uses minimal strut/springs in back that give the hardtail look and still provide a little give.

than stock. Some crafty builders move the lower shock mount on the swing arm farther back or down, to achieve the same effect. Once again, this requires high-quality welding.

If you buy shorter shocks, buy the best quality shocks you can afford. Companies like White Brothers and Progressive Suspension offer gas-charged shocks that provide a better ride and increased resistance to fade—in a variety of lengths and styles.

If you don't want to weld up your own modified swing arm, companies like Arlen Ness, Drag Specialties and Custom Chrome offer a variety of swing arms designed to drop the back of that

This Softail uses a factory caliper squeezing a ventilated, polished rear rotor. The small, polished cap gives the caliper a nice look. Note the nicely molded frame and the cap on the pivot bolt.

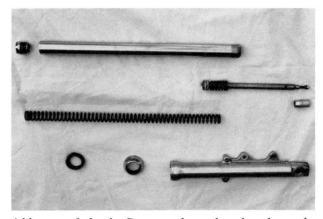

A blown-up fork tube. Some people cut the tube to lower the bike, which means that the bike comes down pretty far before it bottoms out. White Brothers sells a kit consisting of a shorter main spring and a larger top-out spring, which lowers the bike and leaves the stock ground clearance when the bike is bottomed out.

Harley-Davidson. Some of these swing arms offer adjustable shock mounting, allowing the builder to dial in exactly the height that's needed.

The Harley Softail bikes feature rear suspension that is very different than the more conventional suspension offered on the other models. Instead of

Don Hotop
Low and Short and Basic Bikes

Don Hotop builds bikes that work. Low and short and basic. He calls them "Let's go racing" kinds of bikes. Bikes that go down the road for mile after mile without any trouble. Don understands the connection between form and function. His bikes carry enormous detail in the hoses and brackets, in the way things are mounted and bolted together.

Like a lot of builders, Don started out tinkering with go-karts and old beater cars at a very young age. He was fixing cars in the backyard before he had a license to drive. After high school there was trade school where he enrolled in the tool and die class.

Despite the tool and die training, Don always seemed to end up doing maintenance work in local factories. In the early 1970s he was working for Chevron, doing maintenance work, and fixing Harleys at home in the evenings. There was a lay-off, just

Don Hotop builds bikes in the little river town of Fort Madison, Iowa. Don is best known for building bikes that run. His Harleys always carry interesting little details, the kind you have to get down and really look at in order to see.

a temporary thing, but for Don it was more than that. "When Chevron called and said, come back to work, I said no. It was kind of a gutsy thing to do at the time. I mean that was a pretty good job I walked away from."

Instead of going back to work for Chevron, Don scraped together all the money he had and opened a small Harley store. Though it was hard to do at the time, Don looks back on that decision as one of his best.

Though he may not have finished the tool and die class, Don certainly learned quality fabrication somewhere along the way. One of the first bikes Don was really proud of was a little rigid-framed Shovelhead. He calls it "103ci of fire-breathing monster." Painted black, the beast had a car tire in the back and would stand up on the tire anytime Don twisted the throttle. Not only was the black beast fast, it was assembled with great attention to detail.

Don gets real involved in the details and feels everything on the bike needs to have its place. He explains further: "There's no excuse for a cable hanging down or a missing bracket. If you're trying to show off your skills and talents you shouldn't go with a cheap little cadmium-plated bracket off the shelf. When people get down and really look at one of my bikes I want them to find the little things I've done. If they can find one neat little detail, well maybe they'll keep looking until they find another. I always kind of take my time when I'm building a bike. I hate to get rushed. I'll spend all day making just the perfect bracket that holds the cable or gas line just the way I want."

The FXR that Don brought to Sturgis recently is another good example of a Don Hotop custom Harley. At first the bike seems almost stock. A nice orange FXR, lowered and repainted. In reality the bike is a sleeper. One of those where the more you look, the more you see.

The apparently stock Harley frame was cut into eight pieces so Don could build an FXR frame that met his high standards. The great paint was applied by Dave Perewitz. Where the bike really shines though is in the little things: the "mystery" hose clamps machined from stainless steel. The brake lines and fittings that look unlike anything else you've ever seen. The little brackets that Don takes such pride in, the ones that hold the cables just right.

Before he starts shaping a piece of metal, Don spends considerable time with a pencil and paper. He explains that it saves a lot of wasted time and material. And it helps Don to create the shapes he takes such pleasure in.

Don has a phrase for a bike or a bracket where everything turned out just perfect. He calls it mechanical beauty. It's that perfect blending of form and function. The bracket, the bike, that not only look great but work great too.

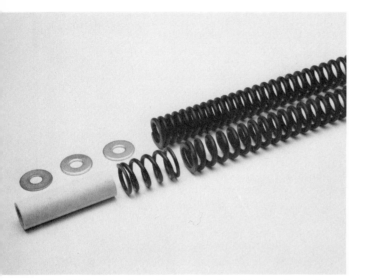

The White Brothers front lowering kit consists of new main springs, shorter than stock and wound to be a little stiffer so they work better over a shorter total travel. Their kit also includes a new top-out spring as well.

A graphic demonstration: two similar FXRs (both built by Donnie Smith), one with a stock fork angle, one with an additional 5 degrees of rake. The bike in the background is lowered but has a stock fork angle; the bike in the foreground has been lowered and raked.

An early Sportster frame. This is Lenny Schwartz' Sportster before the engine was installed. Once a very radical ride, Lenny de-stretched the frame to get it closer to stock dimensions (it still has at least a 2in frame stretch). The modified fork angle was left intact when the de-stretching was done. Rear fender is an Arlen Ness Streamliner fender.

Partly assembled, the ultra Fat Boy by Donnie Smith. Frame is stock, lowered of course. Swing arm, too, is stock Harley-Davidson—painted to match the body.

arm, those hidden under the Softail's gearbox pull on the triangulated swing arm.

This novel suspension design requires a different approach when it comes to lowering the bike. The Softail also starts life physically lower than some of the other Harley models (like the FXR series, for example) and starts to drag relatively easily if the bike is lowered too far.

White Brothers offers kits for both early and late Softails that drop the back of the bike approximately 1in. They also offer shock-spring units that provide better overall ride and handling than the stock units. Some builders and bike shops are lowering the bike by modifying the swing arm, while Arlen Ness offers a sleek new swing arm with a height adjustment that lowers the back of a Softail up to 2in. White Brothers is also rumored to be working on an adjustable lowering kit for the Softails.

Lowering the front of the bike to match the rear can be done by cutting the tubes or by installing a spring kit from White Brothers. Custom Chrome, Drag Specialties and others offer new fork tubes, both shorter and longer than stock.

White Brothers offers a spring kit that drops the front of most late-model Harleys up to 2in. The kit includes new fork and rebound springs. The fork

mounting the shock-spring units on the side of the bike where everyone can see them, the Softail hides its two units under the gearbox. While all other shock-spring units push against the swing

Same bike, just a little further along. Fender rail is a Ness unit, designed to look slick and mount the fenders lower on the bike. Wheels are from Performance Machine, with 16in rubber on the front and rear.

springs are shorter, though stiffer, than stock. The reassembled fork will be shorter than stock and have reduced suspension travel as well. White Brothers claims that this is a safer way of lowering the front of your Harley because the kit lowers the bike *and* reduces suspension travel—so the bike "bottoms" where it did before (with the frame the same distance from the ground) and is less likely to drag the chassis across those bad bumps.

For those in search of true exotica in front forks, some new, "upside-down" front forks are coming onto the market. Used on road-race bikes for some time, these forks have the two major components reversed from the configuration we have known for so long. They're soon to be available completely polished and designed to bolt on to late-model Harley-Davidsons, and offer a look all their own— one that stresses function first and form second. By mounting the female part of the fork on top, the strongest portion ends up clamped into the triple trees. The male fork member is now bolted to the axle. Besides putting the strongest part of the fork on top where it belongs, the new design offers more overlap of the male and female members, providing better alignment and smoother fork action.

The Look: Raking the Forks

Most late-model Harleys run a fork angle of about 33 degrees, although some of the custom models may run a bit more. Many builders feel that increasing the rake—effectively kicking the front wheel forward—gives the bike the look. In this case, the look is defined as the long, stretched-out profile—a bike that looks like it's moving when it's standing still.

The triangular area under the FXR's seat is nicely molded and finished. Pipes are Pythons. The polished, factory swing arm adds a nice accent, and the stock caliper has been polished, too. The small taillight is from an old Chevy, with most of the assembly mounted behind the fender.

But there are a few problems—all of them serious trade-offs—that crop up when the rake is increased past the factory specifications. First, when the fork angle is extended too far, the forks become too horizontal and simply don't want to slide up and down anymore. Second, increased fork angle gives good straight-line stability, but once

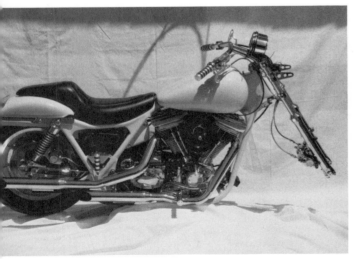

Ron Banks' unfinished FXR. The frame has been completely molded. Rear shocks are shorter than stock and the front mount has been moved forward to get the right height. Fork tubes have been cut, lower legs are polished. Both lower legs carry mounts for brake calipers.

Construction photo of the lengthened and modified swing arm used on the Pro-Street, scalloped Harley. Note the elaborate fixture used to keep everything true and even. Not a job for amateurs!

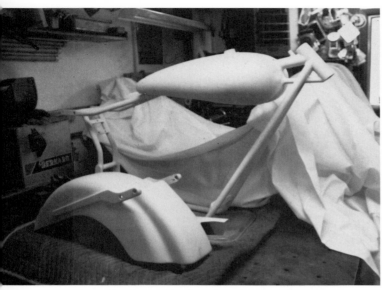

An early photo of the hand-built frame for Donnie Smith's new bike. The frame has been molded, finished and primed. The fender struts have been mounted permanently to the fender.

Frame detail on Donnie Smith's frame. You can see the finished—molded—welds. The hanging appendage makes sense later, when the tank is set on the bike.

Same frame, much further along. Note the strong fork angle, the dual rear calipers and the triangulated steering head.

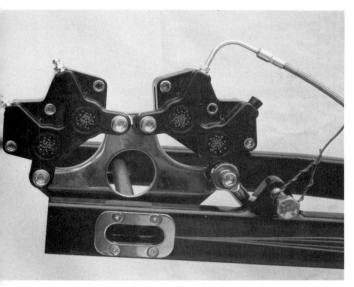

More details on Donnie Smith's frame. The twin, four-piston calipers are painted body color and mount to a custom bracket, located by the axle and the linkage that transfers the braking energy to the swing arm. These two calipers are connected to two master cylinders operated by one pedal.

A recent bike built by Arlen Ness. Note the prototype dual-rail swing arm with adjustable lower shock mounting points. Shock are from Progressive Suspension and are air adjustable.

the bars are moved from the straight-ahead position, the bars get heavy and the bike wants to fall into the turn.

If more rake is what you've just *got* to have, then have it in moderation. Keep total fork angle in the

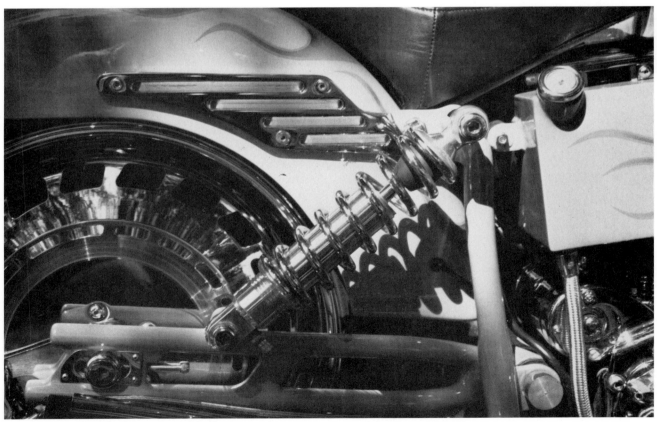

A detail shot of Peter Cottrell's bike. The chrome-plated rear wheel is from Performance Machine. The frame is a modified FX frame, with swing arm from Arlen Ness and

shocks from Works Performance. Note the nifty slotted fender rail.

range of 35 to 37 degrees. If possible, ride a bike with some extra rake so you understand firsthand what the trade-offs are and how the machine handles in day-to-day situations.

The work itself must be done by an experienced shop. Most shops carefully cut through most of the metal attaching the steering head to the frame. Using a jig to keep the steering head straight relative to the rest of the frame, the steering head is pulled away from the rest of the frame at the bottom (it is still attached at the top), and a small piece of metal is welded into the void. If this all seems confusing, take a look at the illustrations.

It's important to remember that this kind of work requires a high level of skill. Be sure the shop that does the work has done it before, and don't let your unemployed brother-in-law do the welding just because he needs the work.

Available for late-model Softails, these Magnumatic shocks from Progressive Suspension offer stiffer springs and better damping characteristics for an improved ride and less bottoming out. They have adjustable spring preload and are available for all 1989 and later Softails. Custom Chrome

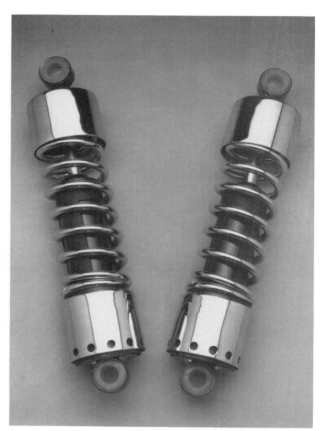

These premium, gas shocks are offered for both FL and FX models and feature hardened shafts and long-life seals. Available in the stock 12in dimension eye to eye, they can also be purchased in an 11in length to lower the rear of the bike slightly. Custom Chrome

Chapter 7

Improving Brakes, Tires and Wheels

A customized motorcycle is one that should work —as well as look—better than it did stock. We all want that sucker to run faster than stock, and should give some thought to making it stop better as well.

Nearly all the Harleys seen on the street these days are equipped with disc brakes, at least on the front wheel. While these brakes are often ade-quate and in later cases fairly good, upgrades offering better stopping ability and a more pleas-ing appearance are available from a variety of manufacturers.

Before listing the latest, sexiest disc brake systems available, a short discussion of brake operation seems appropriate. In particular, the builder of a custom motorcycle should understand

High-tech brakes for your Harley. This Arlen Ness ultra Fat Boy uses Performance Machine four-piston calipers to squeeze large-diameter, ventilated floating rotors. Large-diameter rotors provide more braking area and more *leverage for impressive stopping power. Always be sure the caliper bracket is heavy enough, as all the braking power is transmitted through the bracket.*

exactly what he or she is getting for those extra dollars spent on high-tech calipers and polished, stainless rotors.

Brake Modifications

Brakes are essentially heat machines, converting the moving or kinetic energy of your motorcycle to heat. When planning what type of brakes to buy it might be instructive to remember that when you double the speed of a vehicle, you create four times the kinetic energy. When buying brakes for a high-performance motorcycle, more is usually better. More rotor surface area, more pistons per calipers (usually with large pads as well) and in some cases, more calipers. The downside to more brakes is the expense, complexity and additional unsprung weight.

The GMA caliper used on this Don Hotop-built chopper looks quite different than the Performance Machine or JayBrake calipers. A two-piston design, the GMA is more rectangular than some other calipers. This one has been polished to match the finish of the springer fork. This disc brake is about a zillion times better than the original drum brake that these old Panheads carried when they were new.

Because disc brakes are so far superior to drum brakes, this discussion will be limited to disc brake systems. Unless you are restoring an older Harley with a drum brake on the front and you intend to show it as a restored motorcycle, install disc brakes on the front wheel.

Most builders of custom bikes spend considerable time and money making sure the new bike goes fast. You should spend at least as much time and money making sure it stops as well as it goes. A motorcycle that won't stop with maximum efficiency just ain't worth a damn. And because the front wheel has something like 70 percent or more of the stopping power, spend your initial investment improving the brakes on the front wheel.

Deciding exactly what type of brakes to install opens a vast number of options. The catalogs from Drag Specialties, Custom Chrome, Arlen Ness, Gary Bang and many more are crammed full of master cylinders, calipers and rotors. Well-known companies like Performance Machine, JayBrake and GMA build two-, four- and six-piston calipers, rotors in a variety of styles and master cylinders in a host of configurations. Choosing between this rather bewildering array of options will depend on your riding style, budget and the design of your motorcycle.

Pat Dunn, an engineer for Performance Machine, suggested the following as a means of making good sense and good decisions from all the brake options available:

"First, what are you going to use the bike for? Road racers will need different brakes than

Aftermarket master cylinders are available with 5/8 or 3/4in bore sizes. Master cylinder bore diameter must be matched to caliper piston(s) for the correct hydraulic ratio. A wide variety of styles is available when choosing the master cylinder. Pick something that matches the rest of the accessories on the bike. This is an Arlen Ness design.

cruisers. If yours is a high-performance bike, then buy some high-performance brakes. If your FXR or Softail came with only one front brake, the easiest improvement in braking would be the addition of the second factory caliper and rotor for dual disc brakes." You should note that equipping most Harleys with dual discs means buying the other lower fork leg with the caliper mount. If factory brakes are to be added to the other side, then a complete kit with lower fork leg, caliper and rotor can be ordered from your dealer.

"The next logical addition is a pair of aftermarket, four-piston calipers and necessary hardware, retaining the stock rotors. The addition of our four-piston calipers will give 35 percent better braking when used with the factory rotors. The four-piston caliper uses a bigger brake pad. By using two pistons per pad, the caliper does a better job of evenly pushing the pad against the spinning rotor. Some of the road racers use a six-piston caliper, but that may be overkill for the street.

"The next logical step is large-diameter rotors, good for another 15 percent improvement in braking. The larger rotors provide more braking surface as well as more leverage for the caliper."

Most modern rotors are ventilated, a good feature that helps to dissipate water on the rotor surface and aid cooling as well. Most rotors are stainless steel; polished stainless-steel rotors are available for those who need all the extra glitter. Experienced builders warn against having your

Here, a Performance Machine two-piston caliper squeezes a ventilated rotor on the rear of an Al Reichenbach-built bike. The swing arm is a two-rail design from Arlen Ness; shocks are supported in part by air so the ride and height are adjustable. Chassis parts like these can be painted (use urethane for durability), anodized or powder coated to match the body color.

The front brake and wheel from the ultra Fat Boy. Brakes are from GMA, complete with polished caliper bracket. Allen head bolts have been capped with small, chrome caps.

Dual calipers on a single, drilled rear rotor. These GMA two-piston calipers are bolted to a custom bracket built by Donnie Smith. Twin calipers are usually tied to a single rear master cylinder, much as you would do with two calipers in front. As the vast majority of braking is done by the front tire, this dual rear caliper routine is done mostly for the visual effect.

rotors chrome plated. It may look great, but the chrome surface is so smooth that the brake pads can't grab hold of it and stopping power suffers in the extreme.

Brake pads, too, come in a variety of materials and styles. The pad must of course match the caliper, but it must also match the rotor. Use the wrong pad material on an iron rotor and the pad will cut up the rotor. So ask the shop where you buy your brakes to be sure to get a good match between the pads and rotors. Most new pads are non-asbestos, meaning they contain no asbestos (read: toxic material), a good deal for all of us.

When installing and improving the brakes on your bike there are a few other things to remember, as well. If you are using the stock brakes, and they have a lot of miles on them, then take the time to inspect and correct any worn components. Be sure to check the brake pads for wear and the hoses for any sign of cracking or weathering. Overhaul kits are available for high-mileage calipers and master cylinders. During an overhaul be sure to check for pitted cylinders and caliper pistons, and *never* use

solvent to clean those internal brake parts. Any solvent left in the system will attack the rubber used for O-rings and seals.

If you are installing new aftermarket calipers, use the correct mounting brackets and bolts. Remember, the full force of a panic stop is transmitted from the caliper to the chassis through the caliper mounting bracket. So be sure those brackets are heavy enough. If you are hanging new calipers on the bike, remember too that the calipers are highly visible and must match the style chosen for the rest of the bike. Don't hang billet aluminum calipers on a primarily chrome-plated Harley-Davidson.

Brake Hydraulic Systems

If you intend to replace both calipers and master cylinders, ask the salesperson which master cylinder you need to match the new calipers. If the hydraulic ratios aren't correctly matched between the master cylinder and calipers you could end up with high-effort brakes, or a master cylinder with too small a piston that doesn't displace enough fluid

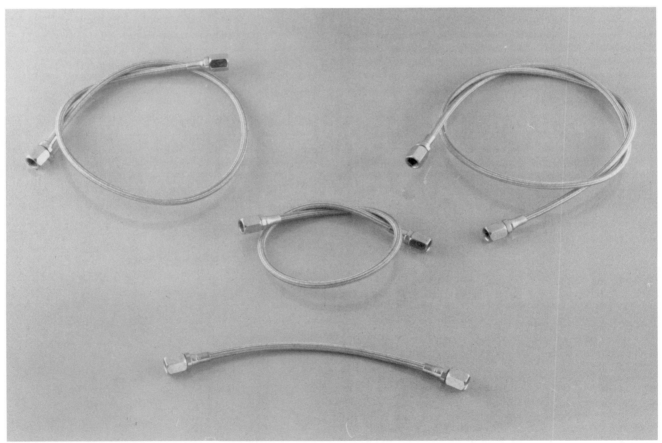

Braided brake lines provide a better feel than their rubber counterparts, look great and can be ordered in almost any length. These lines are designed to be adapted *to Harley-Davidson factory caliper and master cylinder fittings.* Drag Specialties

A variety of disc brake rotors are available to replace the factory rotors. These stainless-steel rotors are available in either 10in or 11½in diameters, designed to bolt on in place of the stock rotors. Already drilled, these rotors are surface induction hardened and are compatible with nearly any disc brake pad material. Custom Chrome

Wheels not only allow your scooter to go down the road, they allow your scooter to go down the road in style. These forged aluminum RevTech wheels are available in a variety of styles. Choose a solid wheel or an ultra-modern directional pattern. The forged aluminum means these wheels are very strong while being lighter than a stock, spoked wheel. Custom Chrome

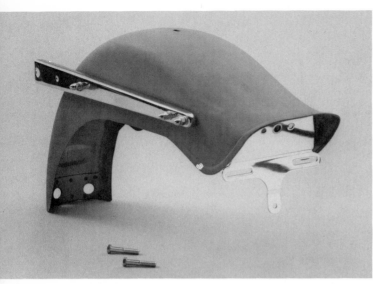

This Quickbob rear fender duplicates the look of the Fat Bob fender and fits a variety of Sportster models. One of many accessories becoming available for the Sportster line, this fender allows the Sporty owner to make the smallest Harley look like a big twin. Add a Quickbob or similar tank and the effect is nearly complete. Drag Specialties

to fully apply the brakes. Stock Harleys use two sizes of front master cylinder piston; newer bikes with the ⅝in master cylinder bore tend to work better with aftermarket, four-piston calipers. Again, check with the salesperson on the compatibility of stock master cylinders with new calipers.

Connecting the master cylinder(s) to the calipers are the flexible brake lines. As the bike ages, these lines tend to crack and may need to be replaced. Because the hydraulic pressure in the brake system approaches 1,000psi, only hoses approved for use in hydraulic brake systems may be used. Builders of new bikes often install braided lines

This Hawg Classic white-sidewall tire will really lock in the 1950s feel you're trying to create with that FLH or Softail. This is a tube-type tire with a load rating of C and a speed rating of S for speeds up to 113mph. Available in a 16in size this baby has a full 2in of very white sidewall. Custom Chrome

Avon makes these touring tires in the stock sizes of 130 and 140/90x15. People who need really big rear tires can order monster rubber up to 170/60x18 and even 180/55x18. Installing larger rear tires is often more work than it might seem. It involves moving the tire over with special kits or even converting belt-drive bikes to chain drive. Custom Chrome

from companies like Russel. The braided lines do not expand even slightly under hard braking as rubber hoses do and thus improve brake feel slightly. The braided lines have a very nice, businesslike look to them that often complements a custom motorcycle.

Perhaps the major advantage of braided lines is the fact that most shops can make them up from scratch in nearly any length with any combination of fittings. If adding new bars or a new master cylinder means the old lines don't fit, you might want to replace them with braided lines. Just be sure to clamp the new lines carefully as a loose braided line acts like a saw-blade when it rubs on the gas tank or frame.

Once you have all the new brake components hung on that great-looking bike of yours, the only thing left is to fill it with brake fluid and bleed the system. So you go to your local auto parts store only to find that there are at least three different types of brake fluid available for your new ride. Which type is preferable? Before discussing brake fluid, though, we need to discuss hydraulic systems.

A hydraulic system must follow two basic laws of physics: first, a fluid cannot be compressed to a

Different strokes, different spokes. Wheels are a big part of the look of your motorcycle—don't assume one style is best until you've checked out all the options. Every year there are more and more styles.

Add a touch of class to the front of that Dresser with chrome covers for the rotor and caliper. Covers are available for most Softails and FL series Harleys, and come with and without louvers. Custom Chrome

101

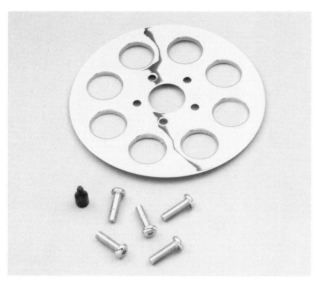

This chrome cookie will cover the rear sprocket of your belt-drive Harley with sparkling chrome. Combined with chrome belt covers, this will really dress up the back of your scooter. Drag Specialties

smaller volume, and second, pressure in the system is equal over all surfaces of the system. What this means is that the pressure at the master cylinder outlet during a stop is applied fully to the pistons in the calipers and not in compressing the fluid link between the master cylinder and the calipers. It also means that the pressure at the master cylinder outlet is the same pressure that is applied to all the surfaces (read pistons) in the brake system.

Brake Fluids

Brake fluid is simply a very specialized hydraulic fluid. One that operates in a dirty environment and must withstand high temperatures without boiling. When brake fluid boils, it becomes a gas (a compressible material). The rider senses this as a very soft or spongy feeling brake lever or pedal. So brake fluid must stay viscous at nearly any temperature and resist boiling up to 400 degrees Fahrenheit.

There are three grades of brake fluid commonly available, DOT 3, DOT 4 and DOT 5, based on

These chrome hubcaps fit the front wheel of FL models with laced wheels and add that certain sparkle as the wheel goes round 'n' round. Custom Chrome

standards set by the Department of Transportation. DOT 3 and 4 are glycol-based fluids with dry boiling points of 401 and 446 degrees Fahrenheit respectively. Either fluid is suitable for use in disc brake systems. There are two basic problems with DOT 3 and DOT 4 brake fluids, however: they tend to absorb water from the environment (they are hydroscopic) and they make a great paint remover.

If you are using glycol-based brake fluid, remember to keep the container closed so it won't pick up moisture from the air, and be careful to avoid spilling it on that new paint job. Because the DOT 3 or 4 brake fluid in your bike will pick up some water no matter how careful you are, it's a good idea to flush the system with fresh fluid every year or two. Remember that brake fluid contaminated with water boils at a much lower temperature and is corrosive to pistons and cylinder bores.

The problems inherent in DOT 3 and 4 brake fluids are overcome by DOT 5 brake fluid. DOT 5 fluid is silicone based, meaning a higher boiling point (500 degrees Fahrenheit, dry), no tendency to absorb water and no reaction when spilled on a painted surface. It costs more and is reputed to be slightly compressible, though no one seems to notice any difference in feel after switching to silicone fluid. The higher cost seems a small price to pay for a much better product. No matter which fluid you decide to use, stick with it and do not mix one brake fluid type with another.

In the end, there are just a few things you have to remember about your brakes, be they high-tech or not: First, don't skimp. Overhaul and repair any used components, and buy new components from Harley-Davidson or quality aftermarket manufacturers. Second, keep all components matched. Match the right master cylinder to the right calipers to produce the correct pressure and lever travel. Match the right pads to the right rotor surface. Third, keep everything neat and allow no dirt or impurities into the hydraulic part of the system.

Tires and Wheels

Tire and wheel choices are a big item for any new or modified ride. Wheels and tires have a major

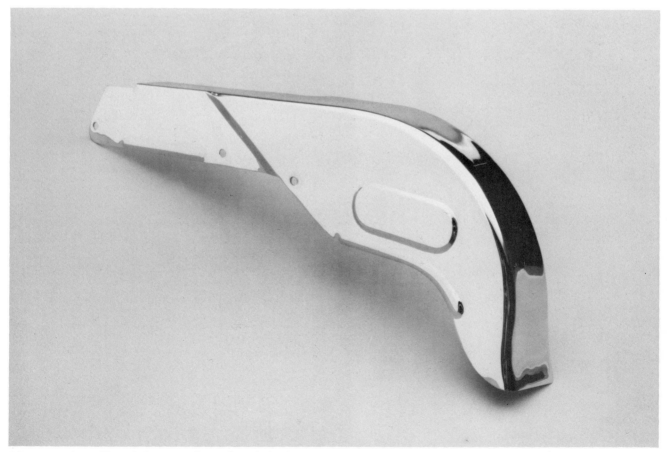

More nostalgia. These belt covers fit modern Softails, yet are designed to look like the old-style chain guards. Drag Specialties

impact on both the performance and look of a bike. Once again your choices will be affected by your budget, and the style you have chosen for the bike.

It goes without saying (but I'll say it anyway) that the style of wheel you choose should follow the style set for the rest of the machine. A Heritage Softail with a fifties paint scheme wouldn't look right with forged aluminum, directional wheels. Traditional bikes usually look best in traditional wire-spoked wheels. With a chrome-plated rim and polished stainless spokes, the glitter is hard to beat. As the years go by, there are more and more choices when it comes to wheels.

In some cases the look of the wheels really makes the whole bike design come together. A modern FXR with wild graphics may need only a set of slotted wheels from Custom Chrome or the soon-to-come directional patterns from Arlen Ness to make the bike really jump visually. In addition to the traditional wire spokes, there are cast-spoked de-signs (many used by the factory) that look great in a variety of applications.

On the practical side, a spoked wheel needs more maintenance than a solid or cast wheel. In addition, the spoked wire wheels may not be a good choice for a bike with a 93ci stroker motor.

Wheel sizes for most Harleys run from 15-18in in the rear and from 16-21in in front. The 16in size is by far the most popular in the rear. It's a size that is easy to find, easy to fit rubber to and one that takes large cross-section tires with ease. Adding fat rubber to an 18in rim is more difficult and tends to make the bike taller in the back—just what most builders are trying to get away from.

The fat rear tire is very much in style (did it ever go out of style?) and everyone wants a rear tire larger than the one that came from the factory. Most late-model FXRs and Softails carry 130/90x16in rear tires. The tire catalogs list larger rubber, as large as 170 and 180 in 17 and 18in sizes.

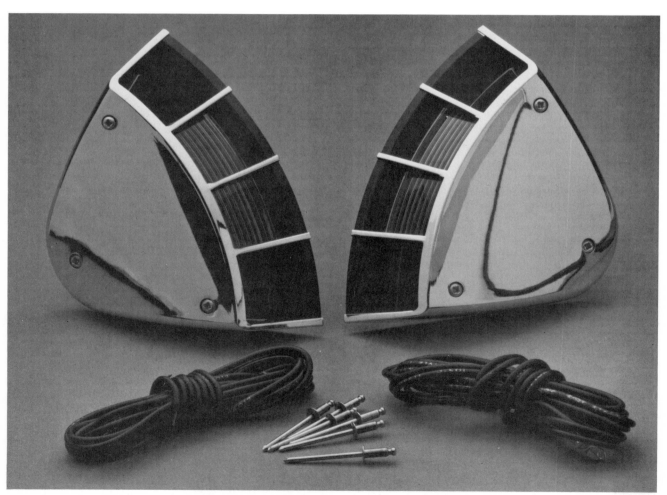

The rotor covers on your Dresser might look great, but do they funnel enough cooling air to those rotors? The answer is these lighted air scoops which fit most front rotor covers. *A perfect blending of form and function, these lighted scoops feature amber light lenses and extra-long wiring leads.* Drag Specialties

Avon is rumored to be producing a monster 190 series tire.

Tire Clearance

The problem is that modern, belt-drive Harleys don't leave much extra room for larger rubber. In fact, going even one size larger, to a 140/90x16 is tough in most situations. Most of the time the larger rubber rubs against the belt—not a great situation.

Riders have been known to trim away part of the belt to make room for the larger tire—don't do it! A better solution is the removal of some material from the base of the caliper mount on the right side, which allows the wheel to move to the right slightly. Then a spacer is added on the left side between the wheel and the belt sprocket. This is more difficult than it sounds and requires an experienced builder with access to a machine shop. Softail owners can install a kit from Arlen Ness

that allows moving the transmission and drive sprocket over slightly, thus retaining belt drive but allowing the use of a wider rear rim and tire.

For builders who require the fattest tire in the world, belt-drive FXR and Softail Harleys can be converted to chain drive. With the belt out of the way, there's a great deal more room back there for monster rubber. Most of the aftermarket manufacturers offer chain-drive sprockets with an offset to allow use of very wide rims and matching fat rubber.

Offset sprockets are offered for older chain-drive models as well and allow the mounting of larger rear rims and tires on older Sportsters, FL and FX Harley-Davidsons.

Anyone mounting larger-than-stock rubber on the rear of his or her bike should beware the many pitfalls. (Get ready for another disclaimer.) First, tires grow in diameter as speed increases; what looks like enough clearance between the fender and

This forged-aluminum, RevTech rear wheel is available in a 4in width to handle the fat tires everyone wants on the rear of their Harley-Davidson. The solid design and forged-aluminum material mean that this wheel offers *more than just the look of high performance. Smoke the rubber right off that big fat slick and never twist a spoke! Available in both 16 and 18in sizes. Custom Chrome*

Wheels are rolling rapidly into the future. This prototype design showed up on a Cory Ness bike. Cut out on sophisticated CNC machines, the turbine design has a nice look. With the new computerized mills and lathes, almost any pattern is possible. Look for more of these high-tech aluminum wheels in the near future.

the tire when the bike is stationary may prove to be insufficient when the bike is going 80mph and the tire has grown larger.

Second, you must be sure that the new tire will still go up inside the fender without contacting the fender sides. Finally, watch out for the wires that run along the inside of most rear fenders and any bolts or studs that protrude into the inside of the fender. In some cases the giant rear tire will mean mounting a wider rear fender and hardware—but that's material for another chapter.

Front-wheel diameter depends mostly on style. A Heritage Softail might run a 16in tire and fat rubber, while a sixties-style Panhead calls for a narrow 21in rim and tire. In most cases you can't deviate much from the factory sizes without running into fenders, brackets and bolts. At least one bike builder lowered the fender on his Fatboy, only to have the tire start rubbing at high speed and smoking all the new paint off the fender. If that fender had gotten a good grip on the tire, it might have locked up the front wheel!

The tires themselves are classified according to speed rating and load capacity. Speed ratings start at S, good for 112mph; H, good for 130mph; and V, good for 150mph (a few inexpensive tires have no rating). Load ratings are B and C, with C being the best suited to touring rigs with all their paraphernalia. Radial tires are meant only for bikes designed specifically for radials (no Harleys in that group), so I can safely advise against mounting radials on your Hog.

When you do buy the tires for that new, improved ride of yours, buy the very best. Tell the dealer or counterperson what kind of riding you do, and ask for a recommendation. Be sure to buy something good; buy a brand name and don't be a tightwad.

Chapter 8

Hopping Up the Engine

Nearly everyone who buys a new or late-model Harley feels he or she has to soup it up. Everyone wants just a little more power, enough to blow off that guy in the next lane. So they bolt on a big carb and rip off the stock pipes in favor of faster (that's debatable) and noisier drag pipes.

Spend an hour standing on the street corner in Sturgis, South Dakota, and your ear will tell you that while the bikes are certainly loud, they don't all run that well. Your nose will tell you that there's a lot of raw, unburned gas coming out those exhaust pipes. It seems that loud isn't always fast, however, and that more (as in bigger carbs and bigger jets) isn't always better.

The purpose for including this chapter is not to tell you how to build a 96ci stroker motor with a blower hanging on the right side. The idea is to help the typical rider of a late-model Harley get that extra power you are looking for by building a mild street engine. Too many riders are throwing good money after bad as they hop up their Harley-Davidsons. It isn't that the components are bad. In fact, most of the aftermarket cams and carbs are of very high quality. In most cases the components are merely poorly matched to the job at hand.

If too many riders are doing it wrong, spending a lot of money for a small return in added performance, then who is doing it right? It seems to me the people doing it right are the people who do it professionally and have been for many years, with the test results and reputation to back up their opinions.

Any design can be improved upon, even the design of the Evolution cylinder head. On the left (in black) is a stock Evolution head. On the right is an aftermarket head from STD with the bathtub-shaped combustion chamber. New aftermarket heads would normally be considered part of the package used on a full-race or very serious street engine.

Terry Flynn from St. Paul Harley-Davidson has been repairing Harleys for more than ten years. Terry has lots of opinions—based on his work in the shop—about what you should and shouldn't do to create a good street engine.

On the left, your basic Shovelhead; on the right, an Evolution. The Shovelhead has a larger combustion chamber with lower intake and exhaust ports. The Evolution uses a D-shaped chamber to create good turbulence in the combustion chamber. The Evo uses higher ports as well, so the path of gas into and out of the combustion chamber is shorter and straighter.

Long a popular choice for aftermarket Harley carbs, the new S&S Shorty carburetors are offered in two sizes. The Super E has a 1⅞in throat and is recommended for use on any size big twin or Sportster engine. The Super G measures 2¹⁄₁₆in across the throat and is recommended for use on Harley-Davidson engines where high-performance modifications have been made. The people who make these butterfly carburetors have one final word regarding your choice of either E or G: "If there is doubt as to which carburetor to use, we suggest the smaller, Super E." S&S Cycle Inc.

In the quest for truth I interviewed three full-time Harley-Davidson mechanics. All three have a good base of experience and are well respected in their field. Because no two mechanics are going to have exactly the same opinions about the best way to hop up a Harley, each mechanic's comments stand alone.

These are the questions I asked each mechanic: What are the typical mistakes that people make in their search for more horsepower? What is the proper approach in the search for more street power? And finally, What would you do if the bike were yours—what are your favorite components and combinations of components?

Remember, the idea here is to create a good street engine. An engine with stock displacement, not a killer motor with nitrous and a cam profile reminiscent of the Rocky Mountains. The goal is an engine that retains its driveability and dependability with reasonable gas mileage. Unless otherwise noted, all comments refer to the 80ci Evolution engine.

After reading their comments you still may not know exactly what to do, but you will at least be aware of some of the things you *shouldn't* do. If this chapter makes you think twice before running out to buy the carb that looks like a sewer pipe in cross section, it will all have been worth it.

Terry Flynn

Terry Flynn is a factory mechanic at St. Paul Harley-Davidson, St. Paul, Minnesota. He got the bulk of his mechanic's training at the Motorcycle

Leineweber makes a variety of camshafts, both for street and strip. The street cams are designed to work well at low rpm, where real-life engines run most of the time. Their lower lift street cams can be installed without any head work. Cams for some applications come as a kit, like this Shovelhead cam with springs and keepers. Evolution engines can handle a higher lift cam—without spring clearancing work—than a Shovelhead. Leineweber Enterprises

Dave Perewitz
Evolution Innovations

Dave Perewitz is a painter and bike builder from Brockton, Massachusetts. Though like his peers Dave possesses a wealth of skills and abilities, he is a painter of some renown.

Dave's fascination with cars and motorcycles started at a young age. He owned his first car at age twelve. He describes that first car as "just something to tear apart and put back together again." The first motorcycle was a stock 1964 Sportster that Dave bought when he was sixteen years old.

At the same time Dave was hanging around a body shop run by a friend of his. The hanging around was the beginning of Dave's education in body and paint work. Before long the Sportster had a lot of chrome accessories—and a fresh paint job.

The rest of Dave's education came in bits and pieces. In high school Dave took one year of machine shop though he says he learned the rest of his skills the same way he learned how to paint: "Mostly I learned everything as I went along; I learned by doing it."

After high school Dave worked first as a machinist and then as a mechanic at the local Chevrolet garage. In his free time there were motorcycles to fix—first his own bikes and soon he was working on his friends' bikes too. In 1972, Dave took the plunge and built a small shop behind his father's house. Not much bigger than a two-stall garage, the small shop had a separate spray booth and an assembly area for putting together the bikes.

No one can do it alone, and for Dave there was always the help and support of his brother, Donnie. As the amount of work increased year by year, Donnie took more and more responsibility. First it was the machining of custom parts, until they opened a retail outlet separate from the shop and Donnie took responsibility for the shop.

By 1980, Dave and Donnie had outgrown the small shop behind dad's house and put up a new, 24x40ft building with a full-size spray booth. A few years later the retail store was moved into new quarters as well. The new store was large enough to have a nice showroom and a small shop in the back.

The projects Dave and his crew get involved in range from installing parts sold over the counter at the store to full-on custom bike building jobs. Some of these are turn-key bikes built for specific customers and some are Dave's personal projects.

One of the more successful projects was the bike that Dave brought to Sturgis for the fiftieth celebration. The bike is an Evolution motor in an Arlen Ness frame. It's long and low and carries some of Dave's great flames, but there's more to it than that.

The really special effects start with the Evolution engine. Dave wanted twin carbs, one on each side. There is no easy way to do it, so Dave and Wayne Loftain do the machining necessary to mount two front cylinders to the Evolution bottom end. The rear cylinder is fed by a carb hanging off the right side while the front cylinder is fed by an identical carb on the left side. The exhaust pipes exit from the front of each cylinder and run side by side along the bike.

The rest of the bike is equally innovative. Sitting on top the engine is a handcrafted gas tank of Dave's design. Long and lean, the much modified Japanese tank arches gracefully over the Evolution cylinder heads and rocker covers. The rear fender was widened to accept some serious rubber and is supported by unique fender rails made of tubing, with the mounting studs on the inside so no bolts show on the outside of the fender and rails.

Dave painted the bike wild cherry over a black base. The wonderful flames were added next, starting with a yellow base followed by successive layers of red, orange and purple. The flames were finally pinstriped in bright blue.

When asked what's in his future, Dave takes time to explain his position: "No one is in this business to get rich. I'm making a living at it, but I've been doing it for better than twenty years. We've got a small crew and they all get along and we're doing OK. I don't want to get rich or open a big store. What I want to do is build bikes, pay my bills—and have fun doing it."

Dave Perewitz likes his bikes with a lot of rake in the front fork and great paint jobs. The first motorcycle Dave painted was the Sportster he bought at age sixteen.

This Accel Mega-Fire ignition module is one of a number of modules available to replace the stock module. This Accel unit features adjustable ignition advance curve and rev limiter. One of four curves can be chosen by the rider, depending on the type of riding and the type of modifications that have been made to the engine. Drag Specialties

Mechanics Institute in Phoenix, Arizona, though he admits to tinkering with Harleys from an early age. Terry has been a professional Harley wrench for more than ten years and has worked in a variety of motorcycle shops. St. Paul Harley-Davidson is planning to run an 883 Sportster in the USTwins road-race series. Terry reports that the boss won't let him ride it, but at least he gets to help wrench on the new race bike.

Here are Flynn's comments:

"In terms of mistakes that people make when they try to get more power from their Harley, the first thing they do wrong is they bolt things on the outside. They spend their money in the wrong places. If they've only got $500 to spend, they shouldn't spend that money having us [the mechanics at the Harley store] bolt on a carburetor or a set of pipes. Spend that money on the inside of the engine, and bolt on a carb and pipes later. Harleys respond really well to compression increases. They should let the mechanic do things, like shave the heads and correctly install a new camshaft, that they can't do at home.

"Other mistakes I see are guys bolting in a big cam and a big carb. They probably get some boost

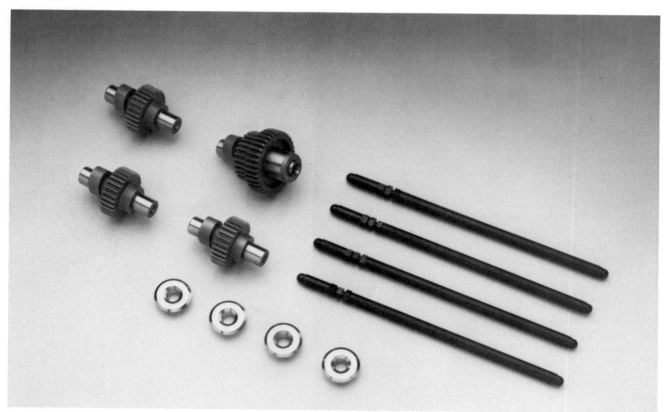

Changing camshafts in your Sportster is more expensive than a big twin, as there are four camshafts in a Sporty instead of just one. These Andrews cams are designed to operate with the stock hydraulic lifters, and come with

adjustable aluminum pushrods and titanium upper spring collars. These collars are lighter than stock and provide more spring travel for high-lift cams. Custom Chrome

on the top end, but they've actually lost power on the bottom end. The cams they're putting in are way too big, a half inch of lift or better, to work with the rest of the engine and to run on the street. They don't understand that they don't need just horsepower. On the street they need torque and they need it at relatively low rpm where most street riding is done.

"They also don't understand that all the parts they put in or on that engine have to work together. If they can't do all the work at once, that's OK. But they have to put together a plan for the engine they are going to build. These people have to understand that the carb and cam and pipes have to work together—they have to choose a good *combination* of parts. The big S&S carb is a great carburetor, but it's a very bad choice for a street engine with stock cubes and a mild camshaft.

"People also want to port the Evolution heads until the ports are too big for good street use. A giant port might be fine if you're running over 6000rpm. But for lower rpm situations the smaller, stock port actually makes more power because the velocity through the port is higher.

"If I were building a street engine I might actually leave the stock Keihin carb in place [this is the newer Keihin constant-velocity carb as offered on 1990 and later big twins and 1989 and later Sportsters] because it is a constant-velocity carb and it is 40mm. I would probably re-jet the carb, but I wouldn't have a problem with running that carb.

"I would replace the air box and air cleaner to feed a little more air to the carb, though. The Screamin' Eagle air cleaner kit is a good choice. The S&S air cleaner is a good choice too, especially for the older, non constant-velocity carbs.

"I would put in a cam, either the EV 141 Sifton or the Screamin' Eagle cam kit. The Screamin' Eagle cam is nice because it's a complete kit with all the extra parts, springs, keepers, lower collars and adjustable pushrods. With the Sifton you have to buy adjustable pushrods because the new cam has the lifters riding a little farther down in the bore and the old pushrods aren't long enough. I favor the aluminum pushrods because they have the same expansion rate as the aluminum cylinders.

"You want to take time to set that cam up right, the right end play, the right fit. Unless they have a feel for it the owner should probably let a good, experienced Harley mechanic install the cam.

"When they put in the cam, they should replace the roller lifters or at least buy the kit [these kits are available from the dealer or from the major catalog companies] with new rollers and new pins. Putting in the new rollers requires a special jig, so most of the guys probably can't do it at home. Harley has had some trouble with the rollers, so they shouldn't take a chance with the old ones.

They should also check the needle bearings and bushing that support the cam.

"In terms of other cams, Crane makes some good units (they make some of the stock Harley cams). The other brands I haven't had much experience with.

"If I were going to put on a new carb at the same time I put in the cam and did a compression increase, I would have to go with the Mikuni 40mm smooth-bore. The throttle response is really excellent and the mileage stays pretty good. If I wanted to have a little more top end I would probably go with the new S&S, the smaller one, the Super E. Guys always want to put the bigger one, the Super G, on their street bikes. But it's just too much carb for a motor with stock displacement.

"The exhaust system would depend on the carb and cam I used. We ran some different pipes on the dyno and found that drag pipes make really good power on the top end but there's nothing on the

This RevTech carburetor offers a number of unique features that make it adaptable to nearly any Harley-Davidson engine. Primary among them is the variable-throat size. Each carburetor comes with three sleeves, 38, 42 and 45mm, so the rider can tailor the carb to meet the needs of a stock engine and simply install a larger sleeve when the engine is modified. Custom Chrome

bottom end. Harleys really like muffler volume, the Kerker and SuperTrapp work well for that reason. When we ran the SuperTrapps we put in all the spacers and then bought the competition kit with an open cap for the end and even more spacers. If I were on a budget I would just drill the baffles out of the stock mufflers. It takes a really good hole-saw, but it works well and it isn't too noisy. You've still got the big mufflers and all that muffler volume that the engine likes.

"I don't like drag pipes, but if I just had to have them I'd run the 2in pipes with the antireversion cones and I would run them with the E-series S&S carb.

"The other thing I would definitely do is shave the heads for about a 9.5:1 compression ratio. If I had the time I would check the piston position at TDC [top dead center]. With the heads off, and the piston at TDC, the piston should be between 0.005 and 0.010in from the top of the cylinder. Sometimes you have to take a little metal off the top of the cylinder to get the piston where you want it—and then of course you'd take a little less off the head in order to arrive at that 9.5:1 compression ratio. By getting the piston closer to that D-shaped combustion chamber it really aids the turbulence of the air-fuel mixture as it comes into the chamber. With 9.5:1 compression it will still run OK on pump premium. If I had a lot of money I might do a little porting, nothing radical or it actually hurts street performance.

"Unless I had a lot of money or was really serious about the engine I wouldn't change the ignition except maybe to put in the Screamin' Eagle ignition module with the higher rev-limiter. A single-fire ignition is the last thing I would add to the engine. And I would never, never convert back to points—it's like trading your Corvette for a Model T.

"Sportsters are pretty easy to soup up [Evolution Sportys]. Cams are more expensive because there are four of them. So with a Sporty the best thing to do for the money is to upgrade to 1200cc right away. Then play with the head just a little bit. The head has to be dished out a little bit. Sportys seem able to run higher compression, as high as 10.0:1. If you just bore it and bolt on the stock heads, the compression ratio ends up around 11.0:1. So maybe the thing to do is take it to someone who has done the work before and let them do it."

Jim Ulasich

Jim Ulasich owns Eagle MC Engineering in Minneapolis, Minnesota. Jim's life of repairing and improving Harley-Davidsons started on the drag

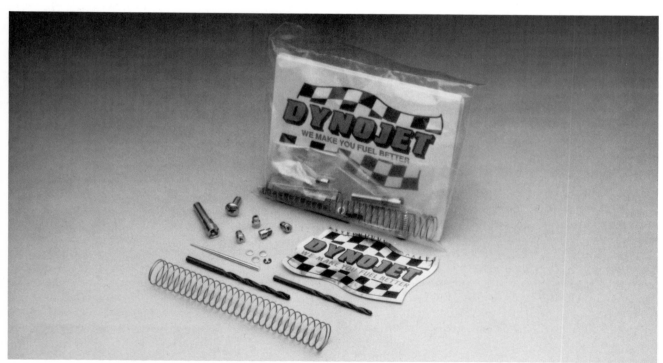

The Keihin carburetor used on late-model big twins and Sportsters can be a good carb for use on mild, street-tuned engines. This Dynojet kit is designed to help fine-tune the stock Keihin constant-velocity carbs. The kit includes a selection of main jets, a needle jet, an adjustable needle with spacers and circlips, and a spring with drill bits. Custom Chrome

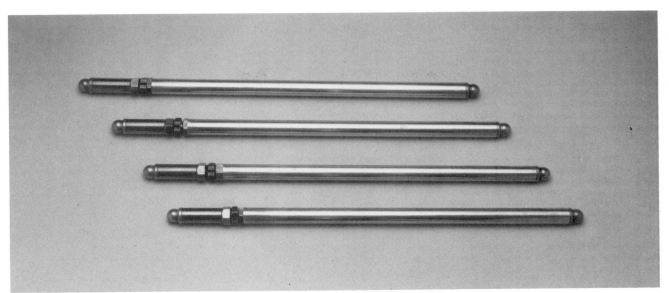

Installing a new aftermarket camshaft in a big twin usually requires new adjustable pushrods. These adjustable pushrods are from Sifton, made from 7/16in, 2024 aluminum—designed to expand at the same rate as the cylinders. Custom Chrome

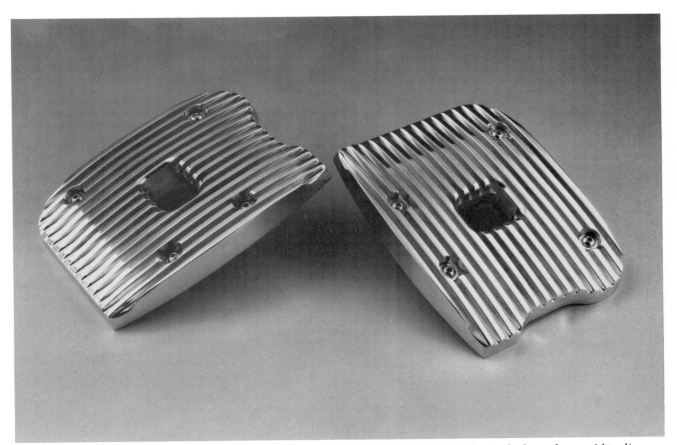

Add a little beauty to your beast with these ribbed rocker covers. Cut from billet aluminum, these polished rocker covers are designed to provide the final touch in dressing out an Evolution engine. The rocker covers feature extra clearance for high-lift camshafts and are said to disperse heat better than the stockers, providing a functional addition to your Evolution engine. Drag Specialties

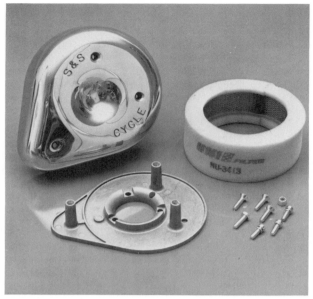

The S&S is by far the most popular of the aftermarket air cleaners for Harley-Davidsons. You see so many Harleys with the S&S air cleaner that you often wonder if maybe they install these at the factory. The S&S is designed to fit Keihin, Bendix, S&S and Tillotson carburetors. Drag Specialties

Jim Ulasich, owner of Eagle MC Engineering in Minneapolis. Jim has a wealth of experience, making Harleys run hard on the drag strip and making Harleys run all day for his regular customers. Eagle is well respected for its flow-bench work; people from all over the country ship Harley cylinder heads to Jim for porting and combustion chamber work.

strip in about 1956, and by 1972 he was running a fuel bike. In 1969 Jim became half owner of Freeway Harley-Davidson, a situation that lasted until the mid 1970s when Eagle MC Engineering was

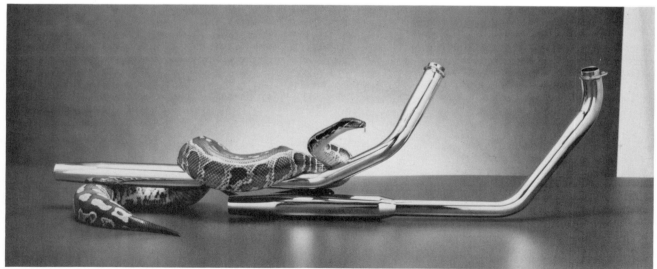

Staggered-duals have been a very popular choice for Harley-Davidsons for many years. What is different about these Python pipes is the antireversion cone used in each pipe. The AR technology ensures that waves do not

flow back up the exhaust system to upset the flow of spent gas leaving the cylinder. AR pipes and exhaust are available in many styles for most big twins and Sportsters.

formed. Jim's background gives him a unique perspective. His drag racing background and flow bench experience give him good hands-on experience making Harleys fast. Yet, his day-to-day work with customer bikes makes him appreciate components that run consistently and give good dependability.

This is what Jim had to recommend:

"In terms of mistakes that people make, they don't seem to make as many as they used to. More people are taking the bikes to a good shop instead of doing it themselves. The most common mistake I see is they're overdoing it. They put a big carb and a long duration cam in a big, heavy road bike. Of course they lose all the throttle response, all the low-end and midrange power and the mileage.

"We also see a lot of people with straight pipes on their bikes come into the shop with "carburetor problems." We often put a set of nonrestrictive baffles in the pipes and that gets rid of their carb problems.

"The easiest way to get more horses is: cam, carb and pipes. I think they should do all three. Performance is in the breathing. How much air and fuel you can get in and out of that cylinder. In about 1988

Jim Ulasich sets up a cylinder head on the flow bench. Flow benches can be used to test different port designs. Ultimately, the amount of power you get out of the engine is determined by how much air you can pack into the cylinder.

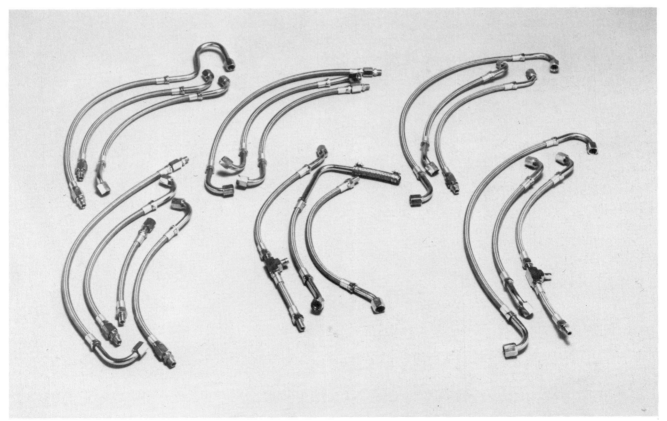

Braided stainless-steel oil lines are available to replace and upgrade the oil lines on your Harley-Davidson. Available to fit nearly any application, these lines are strong *and add a nice visual detail to your engine.* Custom Chrome

Harley-Davidson changed the Evolution cam. In the case of 1988 and newer Evolutions, the bikes run pretty well stock. So it doesn't take an awful lot to enhance that performance—pipes, air cleaner, re-jet the carb and maybe add a new carb last. With the aftermarket cam you need new valve springs and adjustable pushrods. It's a matter of how much money do they want to spend, how long are they going to keep the bike. When they install a cam they should bump the compression too.

"If they really want to spend some money and run hard, then we like to work on the ports and the combustion chamber shape—changing the combustion chamber shape to the bathtub shape. The Evolution heads are reasonably good. We used to modify the Shovelhead heads for more performance, now the Evolution heads look similar to the modified heads we used to put on the old Shovelhead.

"The basic Evolution head is a good design. The Shovelheads have much lower ports, so the air coming in must take some sharp turns as it goes through the port into the combustion chamber. The Evolution head has higher ports and the air doesn't take nearly as sharp a bend going through the ports and into the combustion chamber. Thus, you have the air moving through the port at much higher velocity with less disturbance to the airflow. There are some aftermarket heads that have some improvements already made. The STD heads have a bathtub shape and higher ports. We have taken those heads and done a little port work and come up with some fantastic flow numbers.

"The basic rule of thumb is to use components that work together, a good combination of parts. Get some good advice from people who have done a lot of engine work, not people who have read a lot of magazine articles.

"My personal favorite cams for the street are the Sifton and Leineweber. Sifton makes a broad range of cams for different engine sizes and power bands. Leinewebers are slightly more radical but, in my opinion, make more horsepower. The lobe profiles of the Leinewebers have mellowed slightly, probably to make the cams more streetable. But we still only use them on street diggers that will not get a lot of highway miles.

"Remember, the camshaft is probably the one most important component you will pick and it seems like everyone has a different opinion. Make sure you consult someone that can explain what each cam can do for your motor and what kind of power band you will have. Computer designed cams that are 'easy on your valvetrain' are a waste of time and money. You might as well leave your stock cam in."

Al Reichenbach likes a lot of engraving and detail on his bikes. The carburetor is an SU. The SU (for Skinners Union), an old British design, is a constant-velocity carburetor with many fans. The air cleaner is a simple mesh design available in many shops, with a washable foam insert.

Hardly a "mild street engine," blowers are turning up on increasing numbers of Harley-Davidsons used on the street. A blower like this K&N is a unique combination of brute power and great visuals, and can make your bike stand out in any crowd. Mike Addiss (with help from Donnie Smith) mounted this blower and SU carb on the left side. Blowers are more commonly mounted on the right side. Donnie Smith likes the blowers close to the engine so the intake runners are as short as possible.

116

"For carburetors, I've always liked the slide-type carbs better because they're more efficient—they make more power and give better fuel mileage. We have used a lot of Lectron and Mikuni carbs over the years. The Lectron has such a good fuel signal that an accelerator pump isn't needed. The butterfly carbs have come a long way in the last few years with design changes and sophisticated air bleed systems that make them more efficient than before.

"For very large motors you need the increased airflow and fuel supply of something like an S&S carb. Their new Shorty carbs work very well on the street. The rule of thumb here is not to put on too much carburetor. A smaller carb venturi is good for more velocity and better throttle response and fuel signal. A large carburetor is good for higher rpm and maximum airflow, but it is usually more sluggish in the low and mid-range.

"Vacuum-operated carbs, such as the SU and those used on the new Harleys [Keihin], can overcome the sluggish effect because they will only open according to manifold vacuum. Thus, you can get away with a slightly larger venturi for higher rpm power and still maintain good low- and mid-range power.

"We are looking forward to working with the RevTech carburetor [available from Custom Chrome]. It's unique because it comes with three different sized venturis that can be changed according to your needs [38, 42 and 45mm]. Riders with smaller motors can start with the 38mm venturi and work up as they increase cubic inches or go drag racing. The flow characteristics are very good with any of the venturis—equal to other brands of carbs. Of course, the jetting can be changed and the high-speed air bleed can be changed too for fine tuning.

"For pipes, the SuperTrapp pipes, or the Krome Werks AR [anti-reversion] pipes perform very well with a legal noise level. Both pipes have minimal back pressure and still kill the noise very well. The Krome Werks AR pipes are nice because they're the 'dual staggered' type, keeping the traditional Harley-Davidson style.

"In terms of the ignition, the stock Harley unit used on the new bikes is OK, but if you can spend the money, a good electronic unit with a hotter spark and dual spike will burn a larger percentage of your fuel-air mixture—giving you more net horsepower.

"We dual-plug a lot of heads in our shop and my feeling is that they help most with the larger

Mike Roland, owner of Roland Racing in Minneapolis. Mike is consistently the fastest qualifier at the events he attends all over the country. He turns impressive elapsed *times in spite of being a one-man operation—building, maintaining and running his own bike. Larry Smith*

combustion chamber of a Shovelhead or Sportster. The smaller, bathtub-shaped combustion chamber seems to benefit less from the addition of dual plugs."

Mike Roland

Mike Roland of Roland Racing in Minneapolis, Minnesota, has been fixing Harleys since before he could legally ride them. His fascination with Harley-Davidsons and how they run led him straight to the drag strip. After twenty years of racing, Mike is currently campaigning a Harley in Top Fuel class. Despite being a one-man band (Mike is both rider and mechanic for his bike) running against teams with better funding and apparently more sophisticated machinery, Mike's Harley is nearly always the top qualifier. In 1990, he was the B-Fuel national champion and holds records in B, A and Top Fuel. During the recent season, Mike has been top qualifier at nearly all the meets he has attended. Anyone

who doubts Mike's ability to get the most from a Harley should consider his best time of 7.39 seconds in the quarter mile.

Mike's comments are as follows:

"The most common mistake I see are all the guys putting straight pipes on their bikes. The Evolution doesn't work as well with straight pipes as it does with some kind of muffler system—on the street. The Evolution is really sensitive to the exhaust system. Drag pipes make a lot of noise but they don't run any faster, they don't have good power all through the power band. The other dumb thing that people do is bolt on a great big carburetor without doing anything else, no cam or other engine work.

"Another thing the guys do is throw away that good electronic ignition and install the old points systems.

"Like I said, the Evolution engines are real sensitive to the type of exhaust system you bolt on. It's the reversion waves that will actually give you all the trouble. With a straight pipe the sound waves come out the end of the pipe and then bounce off the atmosphere. With a straight pipe the sound waves run right back up the pipe, through the combustion chamber during valve overlap and cause the air moving through the carburetor to stop or actually move the wrong way. That's why some of the bikes stutter about 3500rpm. The muffler acts to break up those sound waves as they try to move back up the exhaust pipes. The Super-Trapp is one of the best and I think it's because those discs act to really block those waves when they try to move back up the pipe.

"For a carburetor in a mild street-style Evo motor, I would use either the new S&S, E Series

This Bob Walters-built bike has a very clean, efficient looking engine. Barrels are painted white; Dell'Orto carb reaches for air. Engines can be painted quite easily. Parts should first be cleaned, then bead blasted and, finally, primed with a catalyzed product. The finish paint should be a catalyzed urethane due to its greater durability.

A great-looking engine in an Arlen Ness-built bike. The S&S air cleaner is nearly mandatory, exhaust pipes are simple and short. The engine has been painted black, fins are polished, and oil lines are braided stainless steel.

carburetor or maybe the smooth-bore Mikuni 40mm carb.

"I'm a big believer in good ignition. No one wants to spend the money but they should. I would start with a better module for the stock ignition or better yet, a good single-fire ignition.

"My personal combination would be: pull the heads and shave the barrels a little so the piston comes up closer into the combustion chamber. That really helps create turbulence in that D-shaped combustion chamber. I would shave the head a little so the compression came out to about 9.5:1. Then I would add a cam, probably a Sifton EV 141 cam and maybe clean up the ports just a little, nothing radical. My second choice would be a Crane or Screamin' Eagle cam—following the manufacturer's recommendations as to which model to run on the street with your particular combination of exhaust and carburetor.

"For a carburetor I would run either the S&S Series E, the smaller of their two new carbs, or else the Mikuni 40mm smooth-bore. For exhaust I'd use SuperTrapp, period.

"And of course I'd use a single-fire ignition. I really think it helps the engine run more smoothly and develop more power. The unit I like best is the Power Arc from M. C. Ignition. It's basically the same unit I use on my fuel bike."

Plain Talk About Camshafts

Trying to figure out which camshaft is best and why can be a mighty confusing business. The following discussion is intended to help reduce the confusion and clarify some terms. Though your understanding may improve, you should still seek advice from the manufacturer and/or the shop doing the work before choosing a camshaft.

First, let's walk through two crankshaft rotations on a typical single-cylinder, four-cycle engine. Because the camshaft runs at half the speed of the crank, the camshaft will turn one complete revolution to the crankshaft's two.

Power Stroke

On the beginning of the power stroke, with the piston at or near TDC (top dead center), both valves

RevTech makes a line of cylinder heads that are shipped completely assembled, ready to bolt onto your Evolution big twin. Cast from heat-treated 356 aluminum, these heads feature raised intake ports and oversize intake valves. Available in standard and Deluxe trim (with and without hand-finished ports), they come already drilled for dual plugs and have a bathtub-shaped combustion chamber. Custom Chrome

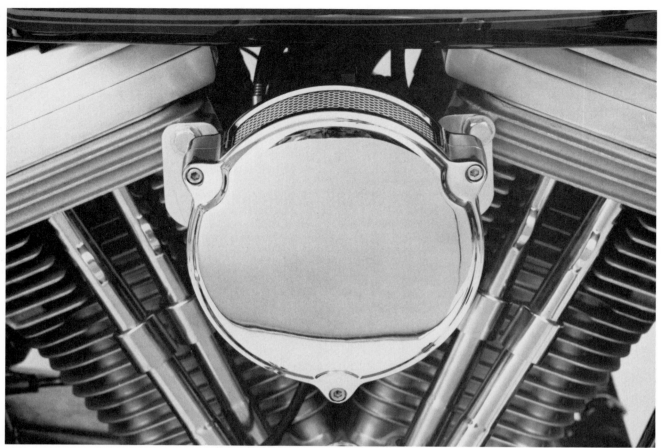

A neat, simple design, these U.S. Legend Dragtron air cleaners are small and avoid interference with the right knee. Available to fit most big twins with Keihin and Bendix carbs, these air cleaners have a backing plate designed to feed more air to your carburetor and a washable filter element. Drag Specialties

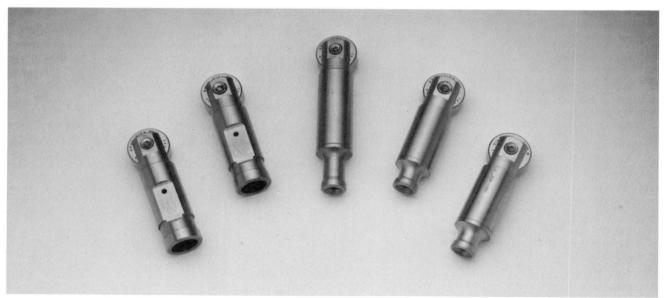

Sometimes it's necessary to replace the whole lifter assembly rather than just the roller. These new lifter assemblies are available in hydraulic or solid, standard and oversize for most pre-Evolution big twins and Sportsters. Custom Chrome

are closed. A spark causes pressure in the cylinder to build and the piston is forced downward. As the piston nears the bottom of the cylinder, the pressure—and power production—drops off. In order to get as much of the spent gas out of the cylinder as possible the exhaust valve opens before the piston actually reaches BDC (bottom dead center). With a typical, mild street camshaft, the exhaust valve opens at about 60 crankshaft degrees before the piston hits BDC.

Exhaust Stroke

The exhaust valve is open as this stroke begins, and stays open during the entire 180 degrees of the exhaust stroke. In order to pack as much fresh gas as possible into the cylinder—especially during higher rpm—the intake valve actually opens before the piston hits TDC. This period when both valves are open is known as the overlap period. Typical street cams begin opening the intake valve at about 30 degrees before the piston reaches TDC during the exhaust stroke.

Intake Stroke

As the intake stroke begins, both valves are open. By about 25 degrees past TDC the exhaust valve has closed, ending the overlap period. The intake valve remains open during the rest of the intake stroke.

Compression Stroke

Though it would seem best to close the intake valve when the piston hits BDC, the gas and air are coming into the cylinder with a certain momentum (especially at higher rpm) and the piston doesn't start to build pressure until it is partway up into the cylinder. For these reasons the intake valve stays open part way into the compression stroke. A typical street cam closes the intake valve at about 40 degrees ABDC (after bottom dead center).

Duration

Duration, the amount of time the cam holds the valve open, can be figured from the previous information. In the case of the exhaust valve, the duration includes the last 60 degrees of the power stroke, plus the full 180 degrees of the exhaust stroke, plus the first 25 degrees of the intake stroke for a total of 265 degrees. Duration for the intake includes 30 degrees of the exhaust stroke, the full 180 degrees of the intake stroke and 40 degrees of the compression stroke for a total of 250 degrees.

When comparing duration figures from one cam to another, it is important to use the correct duration specification. In order to keep everything equal, most manufacturers give a duration specification after the lifter has achieved 0.053in of lift. Use this specification to compare camshafts, not the advertised duration, which may be different.

Some cam manufacturers use duration figures as the basis for the model number of each cam. Crane, for example, uses duration at 0.015, 0.020 and 0.024in of lift for various cam series. Leineweber is the only major cam manufacturer that does not publish a duration at 0.053in specification, choosing to use a specification at 0.020in of lift instead, but that will change with their new catalog.

As a rule of thumb, a cam with longer duration will have more power higher in the rpm range than a cam with less duration. Too much duration on the street will give you a bike with no bottom end, no power at lower rpm where you tend to need it most.

Overlap

Overlap is that period of time when both the intake and exhaust valves are open. In the example above, valve overlap would start at 30 degrees BTDC (before top dead center) and end at 25 degrees ATDC (after top dead center), for a total of 55 degrees.

Lobe Separation Angle

Some cam manufacturers are starting to use a new term, Lobe Separation Angle, instead of overlap. It is the distance in cam degrees between the centerline of the intake and exhaust lobe. Similar to overlap, the separation angle is more comprehensive. Not only does it include overlap information (a

Though not always the best exhaust for an Evolution engine run on the street, drag pipes continue to be among the most popular of aftermarket exhaust systems. Some of the new drag pipe designs are antireversionary and overcome most of the shortcomings exhibited by drag pipes when used on mild, street Evolution motors. Drag Specialties

The old Panheads used a two-into-one exhaust system similar to this Dyno Power system. Available to fit most Softails, these systems can be ordered with different muffler styles, from fishtail to rocket style. Custom Chrome

You can soup up the motor for better acceleration, or you can change the gearing and have almost the same effect. These Andrews sprockets are available both bigger and smaller than the stock, thirty-two-tooth factory sprocket.

For acceleration, order the twenty-nine-tooth. Before leaving for that trip across country, order the thirty-four-tooth sprocket. Drag Specialties

Whenever a new camshaft is installed, the lifters should be inspected and likely replaced. The job of installing new rollers in existing lifter assemblies requires a jig like this one. Custom Chrome

This blower on an Al Reichenbach bike is driven by a belt system and cross shaft that runs across from left to right in front of the engine. Fed by a single SU carburetor, this blower is mounted very close to the engine to keep the intake plumbing as short and simple as possible. Some people like to mount the blowers down low on the frame, a situation that requires longer and more complicated manifolds.

narrow angle means more overlap), it provides more valve timing information than the simple overlap specification alone. In general, a cam with more overlap will tend to have a power band that is peakier and occurs at a higher rpm than a cam with less overlap.

Intake Lobe Centerline

Intake lobe centerline is a timing specification that gives the position of the piston when the intake valve is at its maximum opening. If the intake lobe centerline is 104 degrees, the crank-

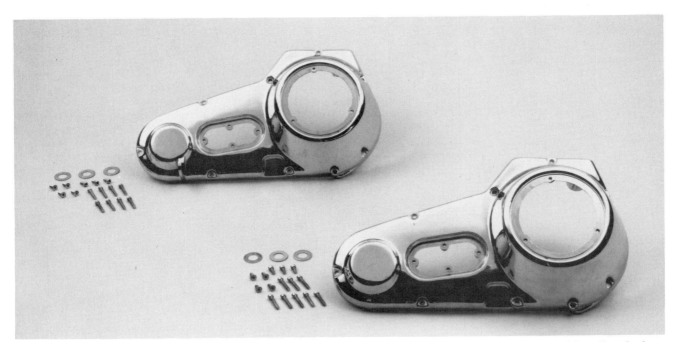

Make the inside sizzle and the outside sparkle (sorry, couldn't help it) with these chrome primary covers.

Available to fit eight- and nine-hole Shovelheads from 1971 to 1984. Drag Specialties

shaft will have turned 104 degrees past TDC at the point when the intake valve has maximum lift. Measured in crankshaft degrees, intake lobe centerline can be compared with the lobe separation angle to indicate the amount of advance the camshaft has relative to the crankshaft.

Fully understanding how intake lobe centerline affects engine performance requires a short explanation. At TDC, or zero crankshaft degrees, the cam has both lobes pointed up. This is the middle (or roughly the middle) of the overlap period and also places the cam in the approximate middle of the lobe separation angle. If the same cam with an intake lobe centerline of 104 degrees had a lobe separation angle of 104 degrees, it would be said to be zero degrees advanced.

In other words, starting at TDC, the piston moves down through 104 degrees of crankshaft rotation, or 52 degrees of cam rotation to put the intake valve at maximum lift. Because 52 is half of the lobe separation angle, the cam was in the middle of the overlap period (half the lobe separa-

tion angle) when the piston was at TDC. If the same cam with the lobe separation angle of 104 degrees had an intake lobe centerline of 100 degrees, then the cam is said to be 4 degrees advanced—this cam would reach maximum intake lift after 100 degrees of crankshaft rotation or four degrees sooner.

Valve Lift

Valve lift is simply the amount the valve is lifted off the valve seat. More lift would seem to add more power, though there are trade-offs here just like everywhere else. For example, open the intake valve too far, too quick, and it runs into the piston. Even if it didn't run into the piston, the higher the

An early Evolution engine moves down the line in Harley-Davidson's Milwaukee, Wisconsin, plant. This engine is quite different from the earlier Shovelhead: Making extra power with the Evolution takes new tricks; the old standard techniques used with the Shovelheads don't always work with an Evo.

Everyone loves the sound of a Harley as it rumbles down the road. Many riders feel that louder is better. There's only one problem and one group of riders who feel otherwise.

The classic Shovelhead. These old motors look great and still run fine. If you've got to have an Evolution, the barrels and heads can be bolted to the Shovelhead bottom end.

lift (at a given duration) the faster it must move in going from the closed to the open position. Moving the valve that fast puts enormous stress on the valvetrain and requires stout springs (which create even more stress) to keep the valve following the steep ramp when the valve closes.

Valve lift is also limited by the spring. A given spring can only be compressed so far before the coils bind. Shovelheads will take up to 0.450in of lift before spring clearancing work is needed, while the Evolution can run all the way to 0.500in of lift without any clearancing. Be sure to check with the manufacturer before installing the cam for any other clearance problems (like between the piston and the valves) or requirements for new springs and pushrods.

Don't be outdone by the rice grinders; get four-valve heads for your Harley-Davidson from Rivera Engineering. Designed by Jim Feuling—the man responsible for the Quad-Four Oldsmobile that went 267mph—the new heads are a bolt-on item reportedly good for an easy 100 street horsepower. Rivera Engineering

Designing a cam is very much a matter of matching the lobe shapes, lift, duration and timing to a particular set of operating conditions. Timing is always critical on a Harley cam to ensure that the two valves don't run into each other. To produce power, air and fuel must be encouraged to enter the cylinder. Once burned, those fumes must likewise be encouraged to exit the cylinder so another fresh

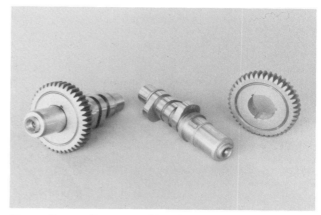

Crane Cams offers everything from mild to wild in their range of camshafts for Harley-Davidson. Of note is their Hi-Roller series cams with a unique cam drive gear. The gear can be mounted in such a way as to advance or retard the cam timing 4 degrees either way. Crane also makes an assembly lubricant that should be used on the cam and all related parts to protect them during initial engine start-up. Crane Cams

Whenever the cam is replaced on a Harley, the roller part of the hydraulic lifter should be replaced as well. This kit is available from Sifton, though replacement of these rollers requires a special jig for correct installation. Drag Specialties

charge can enter. Considering only the oversimplified situation here, long duration would seem a good thing. Taken to the extreme, however, valves that are open too long are seldom closed and there is no meaningful power stroke.

In particular, an exhaust valve that is open too far into the intake stroke (a lengthy overlap period) might work well on a high-rpm drag-race motor. At low rpm, however, the engine has low vacuum (the exhaust valve is open for so much of the intake stroke that it acts like a giant vacuum leak), runs rough, and will probably spit exhaust pressure into the carburetor and/or push raw gas right out into the exhaust pipe.

The cam that's right for your bike will depend on a whole list of variables, including the carb and pipes, the compression ratio, the shape of the ports and the type of riding you do. Getting that perfect cam means asking the right questions and being honest about the type of power you want and the kind of riding you do.

Plain Talk About Carburetors

A recent issue of a popular scooter-trash magazine featured a carburetor buyer's guide. There were nine carburetors listed and three fuel-injection systems.

The carburetor is often the first or second thing owners change when they start tinkering with their Harley-Davidsons. Because the carb is such an essential part of any planned performance modification, it makes sense to back up a little and

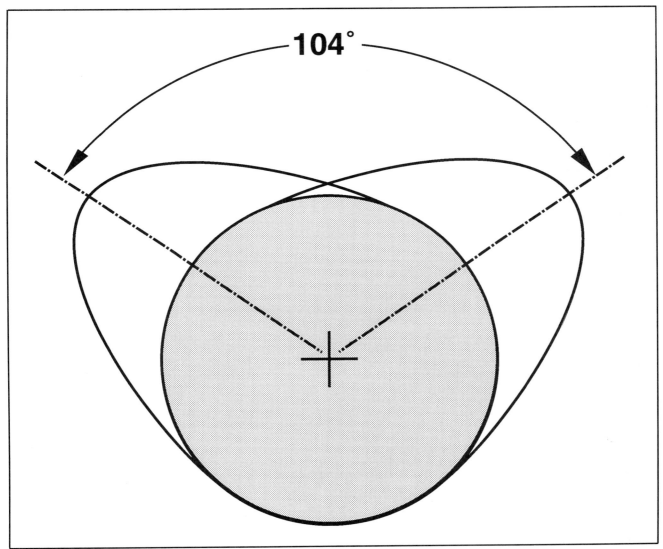

Lobe separation angle is simply the distance between the centerline of the intake and exhaust lobes, measured in cam degrees. This specification is starting to replace the overlap specification as it gives more information than the overlap specification alone.

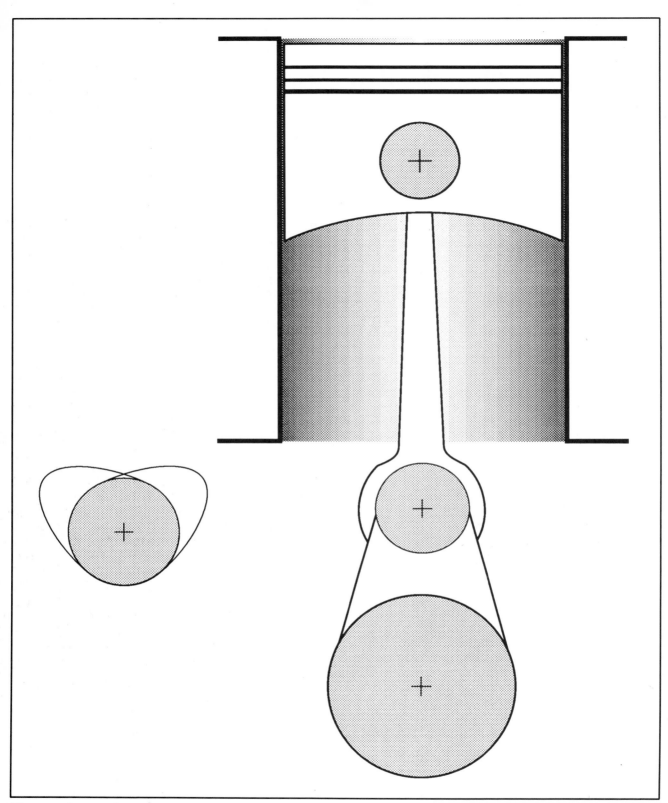

The specification for intake lobe centerline tends to confuse people. This is a timing specification and really has nothing to do with how big the lobes are, their lift or duration. It is a means of measuring the timing of the cam relative to the crankshaft. In this illustration, the cam is in the middle of the overlap period and the piston is at TDC, or zero crankshaft degrees.

talk about what a carburetor does, and what are the differences in the types of carburetors available in the aftermarket.

Carburetor Venturis

At the heart of every carburetor is a venturi. A venturi is really nothing more than a restriction in a pipe. In the early 1700s, a Swiss mathematician named Bernoulli did a series of experiments on fluids and their behavior as they moved through pipes of various sizes. He discovered that when a fluid passes down a pipe at a given speed, it will speed up as it passes through a restriction in the pipe. More importantly, he measured the pressure

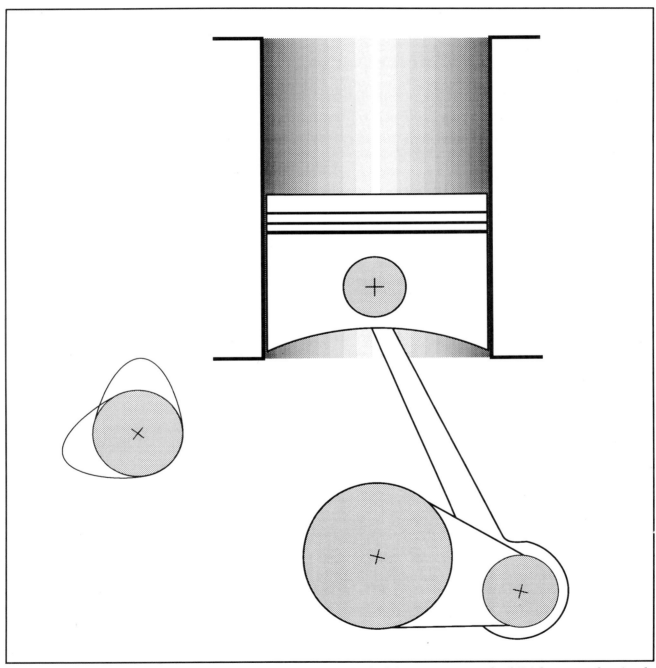

We are dealing with a camshaft with a 104 degree intake lobe centerline. What it means is that when the crank has turned 104 degrees (as it has in the illustration), the intake valve will be at maximum lift. If this same cam had a lobe separation angle of 104 degrees and an intake lobe centerline of 104 degrees, it would be said to be zero degrees advanced.

of the fluid within the restriction and found that it was lower than the pressure on either side of the restriction.

The formula that bears Bernoulli's name is fairly complicated. Suffice to say that the more you restrict the flow, the faster the fluid (or air) moves and the lower the pressure will be within the restriction. Without our Swiss friend and the law he discovered, we wouldn't have airplanes or carburetors or Harley-Davidsons.

To build a simple carburetor you start with a pipe, put a restriction in the middle and bolt it to an engine. Next, you insert a small tube into the narrowest part of the pipe and connect the other end of the small tube to a supply of gasoline. As air passes along the pipe and through the restriction, the pressure within the restriction drops. The small tube is now experiencing a vacuum on one end while atmospheric pressure is pushing on the gasoline at the other end. Gasoline is pushed up the small tube and mixes with the air moving down the throat of our primitive carburetor.

What we've created is a single-speed carburetor with a fixed venturi. We still need a means of controlling the flow of air through the carburetor, and some additional fuel circuits. Extra fuel circuits—there are a total of three circuits in most carbs—are handy for those occasions when there isn't enough air moving through the carb to create the vacuum needed to draw fuel into the venturi.

Even after building a carburetor with an idle, low-speed and high-speed circuit, and a means of controlling the airflow, there are a few problems. First, air doesn't atomize or mix well with cold air in a cold engine. So, for starting and cold running we need a very rich mixture. Second, air is a lot lighter than gas, so when the throttle is opened there is an almost instant increase in airflow though the gas takes much longer to catch up with the increased airflow.

The Keihin carburetor used on late-model Harleys is a full 40mm, constant-velocity design. This design means the carburetor opens to admit only as much air as the engine can use in a given situation. The 40mm size means that when fully open it allows a lot of air to enter the engine. Most professional Harley mechanics feel this is a pretty good carb, one that works well on stock and mildly tweaked street engines.

The Dell'Orto sidedraft carburetor offers great visuals and is commonly used as an aftermarket carb on Harley-Davidsons. These carbs are usually mounted out and forward from the engine. The Dell'Ortos are said to be easy to tune, and many riders will run nothing else.

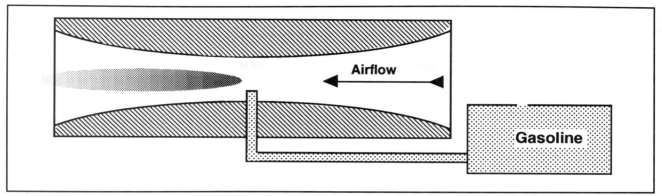

A venturi—nothing more than a restriction in a pipe—is at the heart of every carburetor. As air passes down the carburetor throat it must speed up to pass through the venturi. Pressure within the venturi is reduced, thus the gasoline under atmospheric pressure in the float chamber is forced to the venturi where it atomizes and mixes with air passing down the carburetor throat.

These little glitches are overcome with a choke or enrichment device for cold operation, and an accelerator pump to squirt a little extra blast of gas into the carburetor throat when you wack the throttle open. Some carburetors also utilize a power valve, or an extra jet of some kind designed to richen the mixture under WOT (wide open throttle) conditions when additional gas is needed for maximum horsepower.

Though the basic carburetor theory seems simple enough, the interpretation of that theory can be complex and confusing. In the real world there are two basic types of carburetors available for your Harley, classified according to how the carburetor controls the airflow through the carb.

Butterfly Carburetors

A fixed venturi carburetor—often called a butterfly carb—has a fixed restriction in its throat. These carbs use a butterfly valve to control the amount of air flowing down the carburetor throat. Fuel for high-speed operation is usually introduced

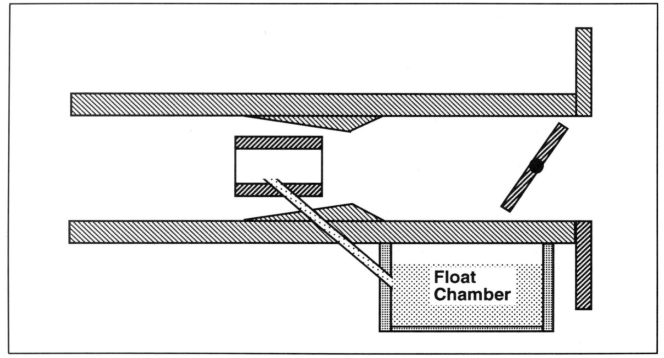

A very simple fixed venturi carburetor. Again, the venturi creates a restriction, the pressure is lowest within the restriction and gas is forced up from the float chamber to the venturi where it mixes with the air stream.

at the venturi. Fuel for idle and low-speed operation is usually introduced into the carburetor throat closer to the butterfly valve.

Supporters say this is a good, basic design used on everything from Model-A Fords to various motorcycles. The S&S carbs, both the new Shorty series and the older designs, are butterfly carbs as is the RevTech, Bendix and several others commonly seen on Harley-Davidsons.

Slide and Constant-Velocity Carburetors

A variable-venturi carburetor is one where the restriction in the carburetor's throat is adjustable with throttle position and/or load. Usually the slide or variable restriction is connected to a tapered needle that passes through a jet. By altering the venturi, the airspeed in the venturi is kept nearly constant over a wide range of airflows. In most of these designs, as the slide is lifted to increase the size of the venturi, the tapered needle is withdrawn

from the jet, effectively allowing more gas to mix with the air passing through the carburetor throat.

There are actually two styles of variable-venturi carburetor: the constant-velocity design and the straight variable-venturi design, sometimes called a slide, carburetor.

In the constant-velocity design the throttle is connected to a conventional butterfly valve. Upstream from the butterfly valve is the variable restriction in the carb throat. This restriction is held in the closed position by a spring and opens according to vacuum within the carb throat. More vacuum causes the piston to open farther, increasing the size of the venturi. At idle, for example, both the butterfly and the venturi are closed.

As the throttle is opened, more vacuum is applied to the slide piston, the piston moves up until equilibrium is achieved between the spring pushing down and the vacuum pulling up. As the slide (or restriction) moves up, the tapered needle is

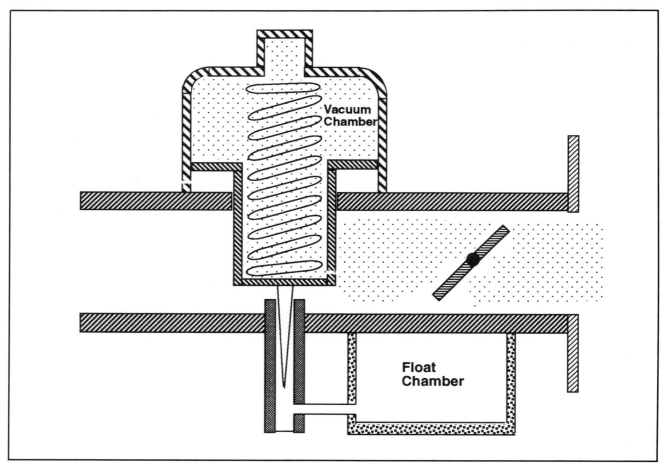

This is a much-simplified, constant velocity-type carburetor. The piston or slide creates a variable venturi, the size of which is determined by the engine's demand for air. Vacuum from the engine is trying to pull the piston up while the spring is pushing it down. As vacuum pulls the piston up, the tapered needle comes farther out of the jet, thus increasing the amount of gas available to mix with the increasing amount of air moving through the carburetor. Though the size of the venturi changes, the velocity of air moving through the venturi stays nearly constant.

pulled out of the jet, effectively increasing the size of the jet.

The two most common types of CV carbs are the Keihin, offered on new and late-model Harleys; and the SU. The SU is an old design, used on everything from English automobiles to snowmobiles and, of course, Harley-Davidsons.

The non-CV carbs with a variable venturi are usually known as slide or smooth-bore carburetors. These designs eliminate the butterfly altogether and connect the slide to the throttle cable. The slide is connected to a tapered needle that passes through the jet. As you open the throttle the slide opens the venturi, allowing more air through the carburetor throat. At the same time the tapered needle is raised in the jet, effectively increasing the size of the jet and adding more fuel to the increased air flow. The best known of the slide style carburetors is the Mikuni smooth-bore.

Fans of the variable-venturi carburetors (both CV and slide type) point out the simplicity of the design. A design that eliminates some of the extra circuits needed with a fixed-venturi design. Adherents of the CV carbs enjoy the fact that these carbs only open up to admit as much air as the engine can use under a particular load. You may open the throttle, but the slide will only open as far as needed. This keeps air speed through the carburetor high and is said to aid throttle response.

Those who prefer the slide, or smooth-bore carburetors point out that by eliminating the butterfly you eliminate a major obstruction in the carburetor throat and create the smooth bore. These people point out that a smooth-bore carburetor will pass more air for a given size than any other design, and that the air moving through them moves faster and with less turbulence.

Carburetor Selection

Choosing among all the variables is never easy. Though claims and counter claims may vary, most of the carburetors offered for sale over the counter of your Harley dealer or aftermarket shop are good carburetors. The dealer will tout the Screamin' Eagle carb and the aftermarket store will encourage the use of the S&S, Mikuni, or maybe the RevTech.

Before putting down your hard-earned money for a new carb, consider some of the following: How massive is the carburetor and how does it interfere with your right leg? What air cleaner styles are available to fit the carb and how important is this to you? What kind of riding do you do? Is horsepower the ultimate goal, or throttle response, or visual appeal? Has the motor been modified? If so, how will the new carb fit in with the other modifications?

It's been said before, but avoid the "bigger is better" mentality. A large bore means slow air speed through the carburetor and poor throttle response. Before buying that shiny new carburetor ask a lot of questions and buy from a reputable dealer or shop. Buy the carb from a shop that can help you out with tuning suggestions and provide any additional parts you might need.

In terms of tuning the carb after installation, most people get in trouble because they swap jets first and think later. The majority of this could be avoided by carefully reading the directions that come with the carburetor. In some cases a rider might need to use the tollfree telephone number that comes with most aftermarket carburetors to get a little help from a technician on the other end.

Fuel Injection For Your Harley

Fuel injection has been offered on production automobiles since the late 1960s and is now almost standard on everything from Japanese econoboxes to American Corvettes. The motorcycle world has seen fuel injection on certain Kawasaki and Honda motorcycles and the BMW K bikes.

Fuel injection really got started on airplanes and was used on numerous war planes during World War II. In the early 1950s, Hilborn mechanical fuel injection was used on many race cars.

The systems generally in use today are known as electronic port injection. Each port, or cylinder, is supplied fuel by one electronic fuel injector. Each injector is fed pressurized fuel at something like 30psi, although specific pressures may vary. The computer, or brain-box, is fed a variety of signals and based on that information determines how often and how long to open the solenoid-like injectors. The simplest systems use throttle position, engine temperature, vacuum and engine speed to determine what the engine is doing and how much fuel it needs to do it.

More complex systems use some kind of a sensor in the exhaust system that measures the oxygen content of the exhaust. These systems can self-correct (often known as a closed-loop system) an error in the fuel mixture until the sensor in the exhaust system says the engine is burning clean and mean. If you think this is really the future you might want one of the systems that allows you to program your own fuel curve using your personal computer to do it.

Currently, there are at least three aftermarket fuel-injection systems on the market. Accel offers its Thundertwin (also available through Custom Chrome), while Budde's offers its own version of electronic-port injection. RB Racing offers another system, one that is programmable at home. Most of these companies use Bosch or Delco components for much of their hardware. See the sources section for more information on the fuel-injection suppliers.

Chapter 9

Custom Metal Fabrication

A nice custom is a bike that is striking in appearance, that looks great and—hopefully—that is different from all the other bikes parked at the curb. Yet, no matter how creative you are in combining factory parts with aftermarket parts and a great paint job, you still come up against one major restriction: All the parts come from either the factory or the aftermarket manufacturers. It means that ultimately you and the biker across the street and the owner of that blue Softail are all dipping out of the same trough.

The way to break out of that mold is by producing parts of your very own. Parts that are truly unique, a production run of one. Impossible, you say? No, not impossible, just more difficult—a lot more difficult.

Making a Mock-up

The first step in producing custom parts is to decide what look you want to create. Like all the other parts on your new bike, any handcrafted pieces need to flow with the overall design. So you need to start with a mock-up, a cardboard or plywood imitation of the piece you want to build. Before you can make a mock-up, though, you will probably need to sketch the part, and get an idea of the dimensions.

The first-generation mock-up may be in two dimensions instead of three, but it will allow you to stand back and get an idea of what the part will actually look like on the bike. If you are building the mock-up for a rolling chassis, be sure to step back from the bike after the mock-up is attached. You might even need to run the bike outside the shop in order to gain some distance to really see how the part works with the rest of the bike, and

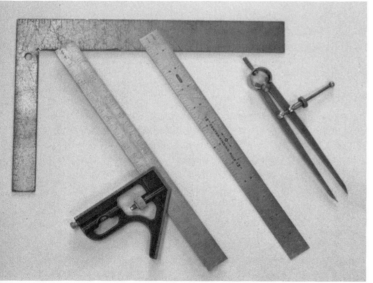

Sheet-metal #101: You're going to need a variety of tools in order to bend that metal into the shapes you need. Accuracy in making a template and transferring those measurements to the steel is critical, thus you need good measuring and marking tools like these. You also need a good scribe for marking the metal itself.

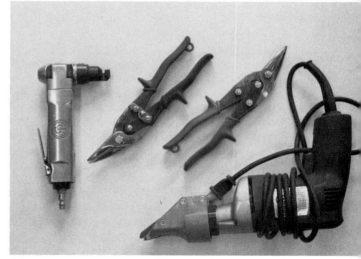

After marking out the pattern you will have to accurately cut the shape from the sheet metal. Pictured are a right- and left-handed snips—necessary to cut curves going in either direction—along with an air-powered nibbler and an electric shears.

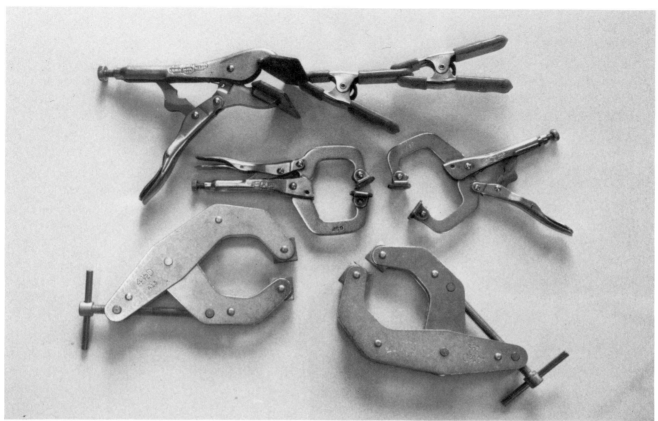

You've got to be able to clamp things in place in order to make measurements, to test the fit of a partly finished piece and to hold things together while they are being welded. You just can't have too many clamps or different styles of vise grips.

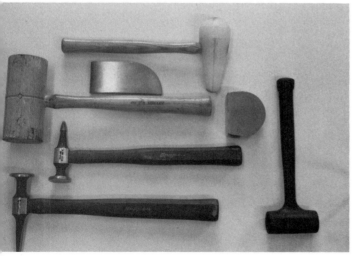

You'll need hammers, too—plastic, rubber and steel in a variety of shapes. You'll also need a few dollies to hold against the back of a piece of metal as you hammer it from the topside. Also very handy is a good selection of garage junk such as hunks of pipe in various diameters—something you can use to bend a piece of sheet metal around in order to obtain a certain shape.

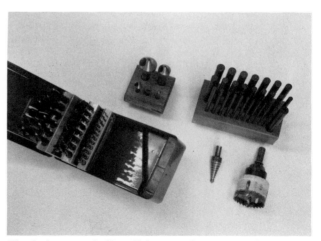

The holes you drill will have to be neat and accurate, requiring a variety of drills and punches. Remember that conventional, double-fluted drills often leave an oblong hole when used to cut light sheet metal. A better solution is a stepped drill. Large holes can be cut with a hole saw, but be sure it's meant to cut metal and not just wood. The rough edge that a drill often leaves on the edge of a hole can be trimmed away with a set of bevel bits. A small, hand-operated punch set can come in handy here as well.

how the proportions work out. Some people go so far as to paint the mock-up so it genuinely looks like a part of the motorcycle and can be better judged as good or bad.

Once you have carefully cut out and scrutinized the mock-up and approved of the result, there are a couple of ways to go. If your metalworking skills are nill, you can hire out the work. Every town has at least a few fabrication shops. They may or may not work on motorcycles, but it really doesn't matter. What you need is a piece crafted from metal; it could just as well be part of a semitrailer or an old car.

The point is, there are probably skilled individuals nearby who can make what you desire, and do a very nice job of it. Just ask around at the motorcycle shop or the local car show. If the part isn't too complex, the price just may be less expensive than you expected. Finding the right person to do the work is much like finding the right shop to chrome plate your swing arm or install a camshaft. You want someone who's good and takes pride in their work, a person or shop with a good word-of-mouth reputation. You also need someone who can build it within your budget. Last, though not least, you need someone who can finish the work when they say they can.

If you decide to craft this unique piece of sheet metal yourself, there are a few things to do before you can actually start.

Gathering Materials

Before getting started, you need some materials to make the new whatzit out of. A catalog from a metals supply house lists a bewildering array of sheet steel and aluminum in varying gauges, with and without special coatings, galvanized and nongalvanized.

In most cases, sheet steel makes a better material for fabricating small shapes than does alumi-

Donnie Smith forms a wind deflector for Crazy John's drag bike. A small sheet-metal brake like this is a handy thing to have if you intend to do a lot of metal shaping. Small units are available from manufacturers like The Eastwood Company. For occasional use, though, the metal can simply be laid across the edge of the work bench and clamped in place with a piece of angle iron and two vise grips.

A trial fit. Experienced metalworkers check and check and check again before drilling holes or welding on mounting brackets. This is another place where it pays to take your time.

num. Aluminum can be shaped easily but has the disadvantage of being expensive, hard to weld (for nonprofessionals) and prone to cracking at the mounting holes.

Sheet steel is a better answer to your small-scale fabrication needs. Cold-rolled sheet steel is more malleable, less prone to cracking and holds paint more readily than hot-rolled steel. Sheet steel varies in thickness from that used to build battleships to sheets as thin as the wrapper on a stick of gum. You need a sheet thick enough to have some strength, yet thin enough to be worked with hand tools. If the parts you intend to bend up are small, like air dams and side covers, eighteen-gauge steel should be strong enough and provide a sheet that is easily worked.

Eighteen-gauge steel measures 0.048in thick. Sixteen-gauge, the next size thicker, is 0.060in thick, while twenty-gauge sheet steel is 0.035in thick.

Tools and Work Area

Like painting or mechanical repair, this fabrication operation will require specialized tools. First, you need a good scribe, a ruler and some machinist's bluing to mark out the patterns on the sheet metal. To cut out the pattern you will need at least one good pair of tin snips, an electric- or air-powered nibbler, and shears. Be sure to wear leather gloves while you're cutting or all the blood will make it hard to see the lines you marked on the sheet steel.

John Frey's bike shows another variation in the FXR side-cover game. This time the frame was filled in below the side covers, then the whole area was molded smooth and painted body color.

Drilling finished holes is best done with a special step drill. With a step drill you get truly rounded holes instead of the triangular-shaped holes that are formed when a regular fluted drill is used on light sheet metal.

A set of countersink bits will allow you to deburr the holes you drill, and a couple of good files will aid in cleaning up any rough edges after cutting. You'll

If you don't like the side covers that are available from the catalog—well heck, just make up your own. These covers on Arnie Aroujo's FXR were Arnie's idea. He thought they might be too different, so he made some mock-ups in light cardboard and asked some friends what they thought. When the consensus came back positive. Arnie had the actual panels fabricated by Bob Monroe.

The filled-in area on John Frey's bike is molded so no evidence of the welding remains. The side cover gets painted in the same pattern as the gas tank.

need a set of hammers, too. Not the standard BFH that can be found in nearly any toolbox, but a few smaller hammers, some with ball heads, some in rubber or plastic, to help in shaping the sheet metal.

Hammers work best when there is a dolly behind them. Besides the formal dolly, an assortment of garage junk such as pipes, poles and angle iron will give you something to form the metal around. Of course, every shop needs a good vise and an anvil, even if the anvil is just an old piece of railroad track.

A good bench is essential in any shop, as is a vise bolted to the end of that bench. A sheet-metal brake might seem essential, though you can use a piece of angle iron and two vise grips to clamp the sheet to the bench and do a nice bend that way.

A welder, at least on a borrowed basis, is essential unless you can make the piece out of one continuous sheet of steel. The small wire-feed

Al Reichenbach
Bikes That Stand Alone

Al Reichenbach builds bikes that stand alone, seldom looking like anyone else's motorcycles. Al says he likes his bikes kind of basic, even though they might have a blower hanging on the right side. A blower might seem an odd addition, coming from a man who claims to like basic bikes—until you realize that the blower is a functional piece, so that's OK. What Al really tries to avoid is hanging a lot of unnecessary "stuff" on his motorcycles.

Al got started with Harleys about twenty years ago. At first it was simple modifications and warmed up stockers. There was a fellow in Janesville, Wisconsin, where Al lives, who did all of Al's painting. When

Al Reichenbach runs AJR Customs in Janesville, Wisconsin. Al's bikes carry intricate detail and abundant engraving, yet stop short of being too showy.

the painter got sick, Al figured it was time he learned how to paint.

Al's entire range of skills, from welding to fabricating, were learned much the way he learned how to paint. Al's father owned a farm implement store, so he learned basic mechanical skills repairing the equipment in the shop. But the rest of the skills came as needed. Al explains: "I picked up the other abilities as I went along. I always figured that if you can't do it yourself you're always waiting on somebody else to do it."

One of the services that Al does farm out is the engraving. A feature carried by most of the bikes Al has built, the engraving sets Al's bikes apart from the others. Engraving is Al's way of adding detail to the motorcycles without hanging extraneous junk on the outside. The engraving, combined with the nice pinstriping and paint accents, creates bikes with good visual appeal and a minimum of gaudiness.

Al is a stickler for details. When he first started taking his bikes to shows, he often came home with the trophy. He remembers that the other bike owners often resented his winning. Yet, when he went over to look at their bikes, he found mismatched bolts, rough frame castings and chipped paint. Al remembers thinking: "If I didn't have my bike done, I mean if some of the bolts were rusty or if I hadn't molded the frame real nice, well I'd just leave the bike home until it was done right."

By about 1980, Al's Harley habit was nearly out of control. Selling parts from the house, something Al had been doing for a number of years, had become a major inconvenience. It was time for Al to learn how to run a shop, and the one he bought was an old two-bay gas station.

The new shop meant more overhead and more work. A full line of parts to sell over the counter and bikes to repair as well. By this time Al was making the transition from long Sportster bikes with Arlen Ness prism-style tanks to FX and, later, FXR bikes.

Al has two current rides, one is an FXR painted black with gold plating and trim. The other is an Evolution motor in an Arlen Ness five-speed frame. The bike with the Arlen Ness frame is the "basic" model with the blower and SU carburetor.

Each of these bikes is different than the others seen parked in Sturgis or in front of the local watering hole in Janesville. Each is well built, very nicely detailed and stands alone—just the way Al wants them to.

Almost too much handwork to imagine. Donnie Smith's wild ride features a hand-built gas tank and rear fender. Note that the fender rails have been integrated into the fender itself.

welders are ideal for this. Most run on 110 volts and many can be equipped with smaller diameter wire (usually 0.024in diameter) for sheet-metal work. Gas welders work well, too. Be sure to use a fairly

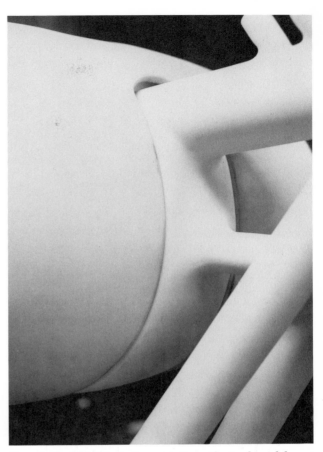

Donnie Smith's bike before painting: the tank and frame fit together perfectly—almost without a seam. This also explains the strange appendage seen hanging from the frame in an earlier chassis shot.

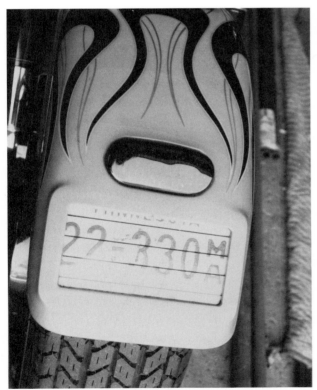

More detail, more great ideas well executed. The license plate slips in from behind—a design made possible by the wide rear tire and a well-thought-out plan. The taillight also has the socket assembly behind the fender, making it less cumbersome than those usually seen on motorcycles.

Just when you think other people have already thought up all the good ideas, along comes another great idea and you think, Why didn't I think of that? This simple, clean bracket serves as both a caliper bracket and a license plate bracket, and it's good looking to boot!

small rod when welding your sheet metal—about the same thickness as the metal you are welding.

Getting Down to Work

After making a mock-up, you need to go through at least one more step before you can actually begin cutting the sheet metal. Because this light steel is hard to weld and harder still to fill in when the two pieces you are welding don't fit correctly, it's very important that all your cutting be as accurate as possible.

What you really need is a pattern, made after the initial mock-up is approved. Made from poster board, this pattern should be exactly the right size, as you will use it to cut your sheet metal. A good scissors and a razor knife will aid in making a good pattern. Don't hurry. Carefully bend and trim each piece until they fit the bike perfectly, then tape them together to see how the whole thing will look when it's finished. This is kind of like the preparation before the paint job; if it's done correctly the rest of the job will go well. If, however, the pattern work is sloppy, you'll tear all your hair out trying to get the final piece to fit correctly and look good.

Bob Walters and his latest detail monster. The custom metalwork starts with the custom tank with its long, lean profile. Mounted down in front is a K&N blower fed by two sidedraft carburetors. All the brackets and plumbing necessary for the blower are Bob's, built by hand of course. Some of these bikes are definitely not first-time projects. But they do show what's possible by mixing a vivid imagination with a talented pair of hands.

A good design starts with careful planning. Here is Willie Ditz' pro-street bike in a very early stage. The cardboard mock-up is the start of the custom-fabricated tail piece.

140

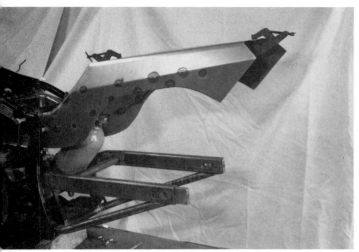

After the template design is changed as necessary (sometimes going through two or three generations), the actual metal can be cut out and clamped into place. Note that the side panels have a crease that was formed on the brake. The crease helps to give the sides shape and also makes them stronger.

This finished bike exhibits the pro-street look that Donnie and Willie were after. Included in the design is a very modern, unobtrusive taillight. The small flip at the end of the mock-up was eliminated in the final design.

Once your pattern looks good, use it to mark out the sheet metal. Spray the metal with some machinist's bluing and use a scribe and ruler to carefully follow those lines. After you follow the lines with tin snips or a nibbler, make sure all the edges are flat and true. A little work with a hammer and dolly will eliminate any waviness along the edges and a file will trim off any rough edges.

The tail piece takes shape as the seat area is added and incorporated into the design of the tail section. The tail section is designed to house the large rear tire and resemble the look of modern fuel bikes. The swing arm is 4in longer than stock, and was fabricated from bare essentials of the stock swing arm.

This is the short story of how a stock FXR tank was converted to a racy, Ninja-style tank. Here, we start with the bare gas tank from a brand-new FXR.

First, the raised center section is cut out of the Harley tank. This particular job was done with a plasma cutter (the latest technology is quick, neat and painless), but a die grinder would have worked too. Be sure all the gas and fumes are out of the tank before starting the cutting operation.

Bend and shape the metal carefully, checking often during this process to see how it fits. If your air dam will be welded up from a number of pieces, use caution as you weld. Welding sheet metal is an art, and the professionals recommend starting at one end of the seam and doing little spot welds every inch or two until you get to the other end of the seam. With luck and skill, the seam will stay

Some poor unsuspecting rice grinder has donated its fuel-cap assembly. With the aid of modern technology, this cap assembly will be transplanted to the Harley-Davidson tank.

Next, the edge is trimmed with a small electric grinder.

stable, or actually pull in a little as you weld from one spot to the other. Then go back and do another series of spot welds in the middle of each open span. The idea is to avoid a lot of heat that will warp the metal. The accuracy of your pattern pays off here—if the pieces fit together tightly they don't need much filling with welding rod. If this is your first experience welding sheet metal, use some scrap and practice welding along a seam, paying attention to the amount of heat you use and how the heat makes the metal move.

After the welding is finished, clean the new part and then apply a good coat of two-part primer to all the surfaces. When everything has been cut accu-rately and welded carefully, the final piece will mount neatly on the bike and need a minimum of body putty to fill the seams and smooth out the little lumps.

Once you have mastered the basics, you are limited only by your imagination. Fenders can be altered, shaped, shortened or lengthened. You no longer have to rely on the catalog as your source for body parts. When you get really good you can tackle something tough, like creating a unique gas tank—leaner, longer and sexier than those that are already available.

And if you're not that good yet, there's only one thing to do. Practice, practice, practice.

Donnie looks on as Al Sperr makes a trial fit. The idea is to make the metal fit perfectly before the welding starts. That way the welding will be easier and a minimum of filler will be needed.

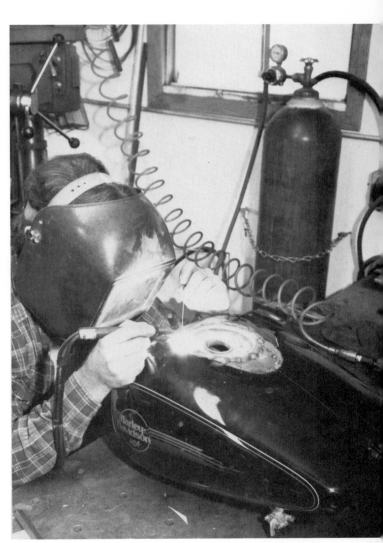

Al does the welding with a heli-arc. The heli-arc is well suited to this type of work as it creates relatively little heat. Caution must be used in this type of welding or the warpage will create lumps and bumps that are very hard to finish later.

143

The finished product, ready for a little body and paint work. The work is so neat that a good painter could just fill and paint the top of the tank and leave the factory logo on the side.

The finished project. Metal-shop projects call for creativity—first in deciding what it is you want to make, and then in deciding how to form it in your shop.

Sheet-metal #202: More metal-shop demonstrations. The key here is in working the metal around another piece that has the correct shape. Jim Perykowski of Metal Fab shows how a dimple can be put in a piece of eighteen-gauge sheet metal. The idea is to work slowly; don't try to make the metal move the full distance on the first blow.

A small, rectangular cover will be formed, starting with a die that it can be formed around. Jim Perykowski scribes a line on the metal ³⁄₁₆in bigger than the block of aluminum.

Using a good pair of tin snips, the piece is cut out of the larger sheet. Then each corner is cut out so the sides can be bent down at a 90 degree angle.

Jim works slowly, forming the metal to the shape of the block. Extra care is taken at the corners to make sure the metal lines up perfectly.

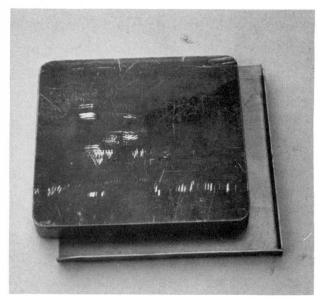

The almost-finished piece. Note how the sides meet correctly at the corners. With a few tools and a little experience, you can make nearly any simple shape in your home shop.

A mixed bag of pipes and garage junk prove very useful for sheet-metal projects (you knew there was a good reason for saving all that stuff). The pipes work well to create a neatly formed curve, with different sizes giving different dimensions. A small piece of sheet metal like the one on the left can be bent into the shape you need and then used as a template in forming the larger piece.

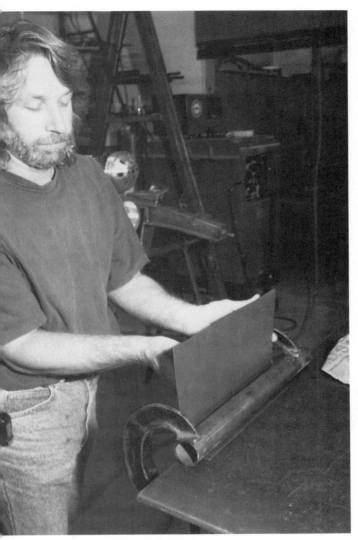

First, one bend is formed around the correct size pipe. The radius of the bend always ends up a little larger than the radius of the pipe itself.

Another bend in the same sheet using a different piece of pipe. By clamping the pipe on the bench, a small "brake" is created. Use a piece of angle iron instead of the pipe and a straight crease is created.

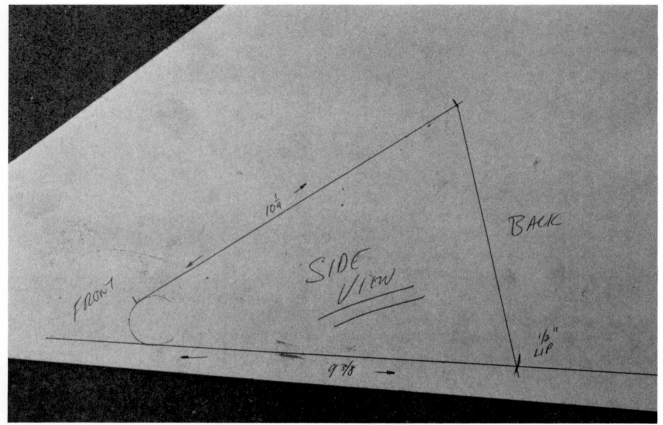

Next project, an air dam for the front of your scooter. First, the shape is marked out on a piece of light poster board. A pipe was used to draw the curved shape at the front lip of the air dam. Always double-check your measurements—measure twice, cut once.

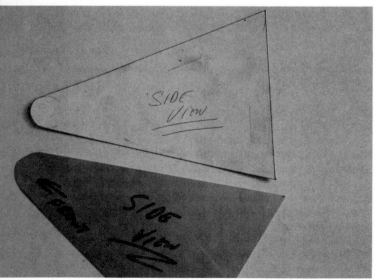

The shape is cut out of the poster board and the measurements are transferred to the metal itself. Measurements and marking must be very accurate to ensure that the parts fit together correctly and are easier to weld and finish.

148

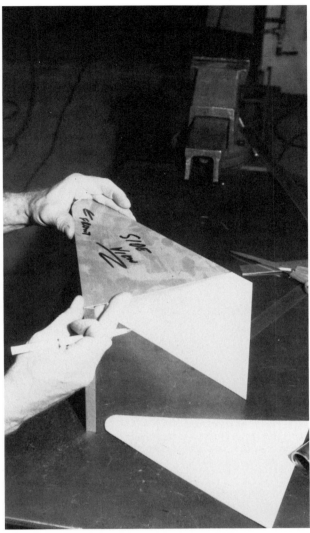

The central part of the air dam was formed by bending the metal over a piece of pipe. Here, the two pieces are checked for fit and taped together. Note how well the two pieces fit together.

Jim Perykowski gets ready to use a heli-arc to weld the two pieces together. Heli-arc welding creates relatively less heat—and therefore warpage. A small wire-feed welder would work well, also. In fact, some builders replace the 0.035in wire that comes with most 110 volt wire-feed welders with 0.024in for improved performance while welding sheet metal.

There are only two or three factories in the world with the equipment for making gas tanks, thus the number of shapes available is rather limited. Custom bike builders like Dave Perewitz are often forced to make their own tanks (or have them crafted by someone else) using two or more old tanks as the basis for the new shape. This is an especially graceful tank design on one of Dave's bikes. Note the gentle arch in the bottom of the tank.

More details. The fender rails on Dave Perewitz' bike are actually bar stock of two diameters carefully bent into the correct shape.

Taillights don't have to be some big housing bolted to the outside of the fender. Ron Banks chose to use this old Chevrolet taillight on his FXR. Most rear fenders have enough room to put all or part of the taillight assembly behind the fender.

A Donnie Smith-built FX bike. Note how the fender rails, the taillight and the license bracket have all been carefully molded into the fender.

Chapter 10

Conclusion

Since this is the final chapter, instead of summarizing all we've said about cams and frames and designs and paints, let's talk about something else. Let's talk about finishing your customizing project.

The garages of America are filled with unfinished projects. Vehicles that are in some way disassembled and patiently awaiting the parts or money or ambition necessary to finish the job. How many of us have an unfinished project in the garage? A '48 Harley or the old Indian or the rusty Hudson Hornet? How many of those project vehicles have been there for more than two years? The idea here is to make sure this new project doesn't end up under the tarp with all the others.

Maybe it's too obvious to even mention, but when you start a project, you have to be sure you can finish it. Here are a few helpful suggestions on how to finish a project once you get started.

First, don't take on more than you can handle. Building a complex motorcycle takes a variety of skills and a certain amount of money. There's nothing worse than wading into the middle of something and realizing too late that you can't handle the heat. Be sure you've got the ability to do the work you plan to do at home, and the budget to farm out the rest of it.

Second, don't try to do too much when you start with too little. Sometimes people delude themselves into thinking they can create the proverbial silk purse from the sow's ear. These folks often think that they can buy the most degenerate, basket-case old Shovelhead with lots of missing parts, and somehow (through some kind of magic) create a truly wonderful Stage 3 bike with a reworked engine and molded frame and custom tanks and all the rest. It can be done and it has been done. But it takes time and patience and skill and a lot of money. You need to realize this going in.

Third, try to stay on a schedule. At least get something done every week. It sounds trite, but when you let a project sit too long without making any progress, it becomes harder and harder to start on it again. It seems to be a special form of inertia they didn't tell us about in high school physics. A project at rest tends to stay at rest. And the longer it sits, the less likely are the chances that it will *ever* move.

Fourth, make a list. That way things get done in order. More important, they get done. The best part of a list is after you get something done, you can cross that off the list. A week or a month later when it seems like you're bogged down in the project, you can look at the list and smile at all the things that are already finished.

Fifth, save the beer until the day's work is finished (or at least nearly finished) and you are sure to get a lot more done.

Remember, the idea here is to build a motorcycle that is all yours, that has your signature on it. A machine that you can take pride in, that makes you feel good when you ride it. Anyone with enough money can roll down to the Harley-Davidson dealer and come out with a new or used motorcycle.

Building a bike takes more than money. It takes careful thought and the desire to build one a little different and a lot better than the factory did. It takes a variety of skills, most of which are learned after years of practice. It takes drive and stamina to get through the low points that occur in any project.

When you're all done, you've built something new. With time and energy and skill and money, you've built this motorcycle. Over the course of six months or a year, you've built the best, the cleanest, the sexiest bike you know how.

And you should be damn proud of that accomplishment.

Safe Disposal of Chemicals and Parts

One of the real problems of doing your own motorcycle customizing is what to do with the junk and poisonous fluids you inevitably generate. Everybody knows these days that two of our largest environmental problems are the related ills of landfill overuse and groundwater contamination. Unfortunately, our interest in environmental problems far outstrips our ability to find answers to them right now.

Some areas have remarkably advanced programs for disposal of hazardous waste, but most locales don't. Your first step in being a responsible garbage maker will have to be doing some of your own research. The city or county listings in your telephone blue pages will have an entry for Waste Disposal, Hazardous Waste Management or something similar. Don't expect to get many answers the first time—it can be a real trick to finally find the right outfit, since there are still no uniform rules across the country for waste management.

There are, however, hazardous waste disposal sites and procedures for every location—it just may be one heck of a long way off, and your local government may not have heard about it yet. If you come across a situation like this, it'll be your ironic duty to find the answers yourself and educate your leaders.

If you strike out with the government at first, call around to local garages, body shops, and restoration specialists; they're required by law to dispose of toxics in an organized manner, so they should be helpful.

Disposal of Chemicals

The best rule of thumb as you work with chemicals and fluids is to remember that if you can smell it, it's bad news. And the stronger the odor the more dangerous it is, both to your immediate health and to the atmosphere and water table. Cleaners, paints, and all oil-derived liquids are the big things to watch out for. Dumped carelessly by the wayside, these toxic chemicals will quickly enter the water cycle and come back to haunt everybody.

The easiest solution, of course, is not to make any more of these wastes than necessary in the first place. Except for motor oil, the greatest volume of volatiles is generated by cleaning, not the actual changing of a motorcycle's fluids. It's best to start off with the mildest cleaners possible at first—soap and water can, in fact, do a lot of work—not just for the environment's sake but because these are also the easiest on the motorcycle itself.

You'll inevitably generate some hazardous materials no matter what you do, however. Things like spray cleaners and naphtha, for example—real health and environmental nightmares—are just too convenient to realistically swear off completely. The trick is simply to catch as much of these fluids as possible after use, and to keep them tightly covered in glass or metal containers until you can safely get rid of them. Leaving pans of cleaners uncovered sends these toxins directly into the atmosphere through evaporation, so keep them covered, always.

Caked grease and ruined rags should also be kept tightly wrapped up in a cool place and disposed of along with actual fluids—they're simply volatiles that are currently trapped in solid form.

All toxics should be kept separated since cross contamination simply makes the disposal issue harder. Motor oil, for example, can actually be recycled and used as fuel for ships and other things. If it's contaminated with minute traces of brake fluid, though, the entire batch in the collection tank will be ruined.

Disposal of Parts

Actual pieces of mechanical junk are generally more of a pain than a danger to dispose of, assuming that the pieces aren't filled with fluid or that particularly greasy, metal parts will sit happily inert in a landfill and actually decompose over time, albeit often a long time. If possible, you should bring big metal parts to a local junkyard; often yards will accept these pieces and use them for their scrap value. Smaller metal pieces, well, there's not much more you can do than to throw them away. The residual grease and oil won't make the local dump an ideal whooping crane nesting site, but at this point in time there aren't a lot of alternatives.

The same goes for plastic and small rubber parts, which actually do release a number of carcinogenic chemicals as, or if, they decompose. Again, though, until a coherent method of disposal is hit on, you don't have a lot of choice here but to throw them out.

Tires, on the other hand, are so well known as a dumping hazard that standards and methods for their disposal have been developed. Generally, the response has simply been to tell people that they can't dump their tires here—which ultimately is the wrong answer, since many people just get frustrated and toss them by the side of the road or in a vacant lot.

A relatively recent and common development are mandatory tire buy-back laws; some areas have regulations that force tire dealers to accept used tires for disposal, usually with a small fee attached. Though there's no really good way for the dealer to get rid of the tires either, at least the problem is narrowed down to one source instead of many. Look into it.

Since regulatory agencies are currently far behind the scale of the waste problem, something else I encourage you to do is start making some noise about getting a comprehensive disposal plan developed for your city or county. Grass-roots organizations have formed in most places to look at the issue, and motorcycle enthusiasts need to be involved. We're the ones making a lot of the problems, so we'll need to be the ones helping to sort them out.

Parts Sources

Listed below are addresses of the parts and service companies mentioned in the text.

Accel Performance Products
Box 142
Branford, CT 06405
  Accel makes a variety of performance products, including electronic fuel injection for Evolution Big Twins.

Al Reichenbach
AJR Customs
1001 Beloit Avenue
Janesville, WI 53546
  Al runs a shop in Janesville where he paints, repairs and customizes Harley-Davidsons, and sells a complete line of parts as well.

Arlen Ness
Arlen's Motorcycle Accessories
16520 East 14th Street
San Leandro, CA 94578
  In addition to designing the bikes they are so well known for, Arlen and Cory Ness run a large Harley store. Their fine inventory of parts—both standard Harley maintenance items and their own line of Arlen Ness parts—is available in the store or by mail.

Budde's Custom Motorcycles
15640 East 14th Street
San Leandro, CA 94578
  Budde's too has a new fuel-injection system to fit all models of Harley-Davidson.

Classic Motorbooks/Motorbooks International
PO Box 1
Osceola, WI 54020
800-826-6600
  Publisher and distributor of motorcycle, automobile and aviation books. Mail-order catalog is available, which includes numerous Harley-David-son titles, from photographic histories to restoration books.

Crane Cams
530 Fentress Boulevard
Daytona Beach, FL 32114
  Crane camshafts are among the best known for both two- and four-wheeled horsepower junkies. Crane makes a wide variety of camshafts as well as push rods, tappets and rocker arms.

Custom Chrome
1 Jacqueline Court
Morgan Hill, CA 95037
  Custom Chrome is one of the largest Harley aftermarket parts organizations in the world. Its current catalog is nearly 600 pages long and includes everything from RevTech carburetors to Avon tires and chrome chain guards.

Dave Perewitz
Cycle Fabrications
909 North Main Street
Brockton, MA 02401
  Dave Perewitz builds wonderful Harleys—often highlighted by one of his great paint jobs. In addition to bike building, Dave runs a full-service parts and repair shop in Brockton, Massachusetts.

Don Hotop
Don's Speed and Custom
2613 Avenue L
Fort Madison, IA 52627
  Tucked away in the little river town of Fort Madison is Don's Speed and Custom. Out of Don's shop come some sanitary and well-detailed custom Harleys as well as some innovative custom parts.

Donnie Smith
2117 97th Avenue North
Brooklyn Park, MN 55444
  Operating out of a small shop, Donnie Smith builds serious custom motorcycles. With a wealth

of experience with Harleys, Donnie builds beautiful bikes in a variety of styles.

Drag Specialties
9839 West 69th Street
Eden Prairie, MN 55344

A large Harley aftermarket company, Drag Specialties parts can be found in many locations, or ordered by mail. Their catalog runs the gamut from soup to nuts—from connecting rods to Arlen Ness dress-up and customizing goodies.

DS Specialties
3013 Lyndale Avenue South
Minneapolis, MN 55408

Not to be confused with Drag Specialties, since you will want to know of both sources. DS Specialties, owned by Peter Cottrell, offers the midwestern Harley rider a full-service department for nearly any repair as well as a well-stocked assortment of parts.

Eagle MC Engineering
1837 East Lake Street
Minneapolis, MN 55407

Eagle MC Engineering, run by Jim Ulasich, is a well-established Harley-Davidson repair facility. Eagle is known both for its dependable service and repair and also for its head and porting work.

The Eastwood Company
580 Lancaster Avenue
Box 296
Malvern, PA 19355

Eastwood offers a wonderful array of tools and equipment intended for the home shop. Its catalog lists everything from a mini sandblaster to hammers and dollies. Whether you need a welder, a die grinder or a special hand file, Eastwood probably has it in its catalog.

Gary Bang Cycle Products
8501 Canoga Avenue
Canoga Park, CA 91304

Gary Bang runs an aftermarket Harley parts company with a catalog listing hundreds of items. Most of the parts fall into the maintenance and repair category.

House of Kolor
2521 27th Avenue South
Minneapolis, MN 55406

Jon Kosmoski's House of Kolor offers *the* custom paint products for painting custom motorcycles and cars. The product line includes both acrylic lacquer and urethane products in a mind-boggling array of colors.

Ken's Metal Finishing
2323 Emerson Avenue North
Minneapolis, MN 55411

Operated by three brothers, Ken's is run the old-fashioned way—each part is handled by hand. In addition to straight chrome plating, Ken's does some special nickel and brass plating.

Leineweber Enterprises
17579 Mesa Road
Unit B-1
Hesperia, CA 92345

Leineweber cams have long been favorites on the strip. The expanded product line with more cams for the street means Leineweber now has a cam to fit nearly any need, from radical Shovelheads to streetable Evolutions.

Lenny Schwartz
Krazy Kolors Lettering and Design
453 West Seventh Street
St. Paul, MN 55102

Lenny paints everything from motorcycles to Kennworth trucks—though the work he enjoys most is pinstriping Harley-Davidsons in a variety of colors and styles.

Mallard Teal
Payne Avenue Body Shop
860 Payne Avenue
St. Paul, MN 55101

Mallard runs a body shop that does everything from wreck repair to wild flame jobs. The body shop helps pay the overhead on the new downdraft paint booth where Mallard exercises his special talent for custom paint jobs.

Metal Fab
1453 91st Avenue NE
Blaine, MN 55434

Quality metal fabrication on both two- and four-wheeled customs.

PPG Finishes
19699 Progress Drive
Strongsville, OH 44136

In addition to its full line of OEM type paints, PPG offers is Radiance Custom Finishing Systems. These paints include base coat/candy coat, pearls and top coat/clear coat systems in a wide range of colors, in both urethane or acrylic lacquer.

RB Racing
1625 West 134th Street
Gardena, CA 90249

RB Racing offers a new, closed-loop programmable fuel-injection system for all Evolution Harleys.

Rivera Engineering
6416 South Western Avenue
Whittier, CA 90606

Manufacturers of the unique, four-valve heads for Harley-Davidsons, Rivera offers the head kits in five stages—from strong street to awesome competition. Rivera also offers its own anti-reversion exhaust systems for use with the four-valve heads.

St. Paul Harley-Davidson
949 Geneva Avenue North
St. Paul, MN 55128

St. Paul Harley is a relatively new dealership owned and run by Bob Crawford. Bob raced Harleys for more than twenty years before opening the dealership. Anyone who stops by will find a very neat operation and a well-run service department.

S&S Cycle
Box 215
Viola, WI 54664

Manufacturers of the number one, most popular air cleaner, S&S is also the manufacturer of the new Shorty series carbs for Harley-Davidsons and a variety of large-displacement engine components to boot.

Sifton Motorcycle Products
943 Bransten Road
San Carlos, CA 94070

Another well-known camshaft manufacturer, Sifton makes camshafts for both street and strip, as well as a full line of valvetrain components.

Twin Town Street Rods
209 Ryan Drive
St. Paul, MN 55117

Tom Rad does more than build street rods, he paints motorcycles as well. His work is first-rate and the approach is often unique.

White Brothers
14241 Commerce Drive
Garden Grove, CA 92643

White Brothers, best known as the manufacturer of high-quality suspension components for both American and "other" types of motorcycles, also handle aftermarket carburetors, exhaust systems and a variety of high-performance parts.

Recommended Books

Here are several other books on Harley-Davidsons and other American motorcycles you may want to check out. They are all available from Classic Motorbooks/Motorbooks International at PO Box 1, Osceola, WI 54020 or by calling 800-826-6600.

Arlen Ness: Master Harley Customizer by Timothy Remus. A full-color history of Arlen Ness' work with features on his greatest custom motorcycles. An essential gallery of ideas.

The Big Book of Harley-Davidson by Thomas C. Bolfert. Published by The Motor Company, this is a large, hardbound, colorful history of the role Harley-Davidson has played in America's history.

Illustrated Harley-Davidson Buyer's Guide by Allan Girdler. Model-by-model description and history of all the postwar Harleys.

Harley-Davidson Photographic History by Wolfgang Wiesner. Great paperback B&W and color photo history of The Motor Company.

Inside Harley-Davidson by Jerry Hatfield. A detailed, technical engineering of the great early Harley-Davidsons 1930-1945.

Harley-Davidson XR-750 by Allan Girdler. The complete history of the XR-750 on the dirt tracks, road racing and on the street.

Harley Racers by Allan Girdler. Detailed history of all the great Harley-Davidson racing motorcycles.

Illustrated Indian Motorcycle Buyer's Guide by Jerry Hatfield. Model-by-model description and history of all the Iron Redskins.

Index